From
Saginaw
to Srinagar

Marilyn C. Murphy

From Saginaw to Srinagar

My Journey from
the Familiar to the Faraway

Advantage | Books

Published by Advantage Books, Charleston, South Carolina.
An imprint of Advantage Media.

ADVANTAGE is a registered trademark, and the Advantage colophon is a trademark of Advantage Media Group, Inc.

Printed in the United States of America.

10 9 8 7 6 5 4 3 2 1

ISBN: 979-8-89188-113-6 (Paperback)
ISBN: 979-8-89188-114-3 (eBook)

Library of Congress Control Number: 2024910683

Cover design by Megan Elger.
Layout design by Lance Buckley.

This publication is designed to provide accurate and authoritative information in regard to the subject matter covered. It is sold with the understanding that the publisher is not engaged in rendering legal, accounting, or other professional services. If legal advice or other expert assistance is required, the services of a competent professional person should be sought.

Advantage Books is an imprint of Advantage Media Group. Advantage Media helps busy entrepreneurs, CEOs, and leaders write and publish a book to grow their business and become the authority in their field. Advantage authors comprise an exclusive community of industry professionals, idea-makers, and thought leaders. For more information go to **advantagemedia.com**.

It's been a long road,
but I'm now at the end,
there are SO many people
to whom thanks I extend!

With Gratitude to...

Scott Gibb, world's greatest husband and bestest friend.

Barbara Nehls-Lowe, who inspired me
and invited me to the Philippines.

Herb Medrow, who believed in me when I
knew almost nothing about business.

Gabriel Haigazian and my talented team who continue
my legacy since I've retired, and to my loyal **WOWees**
who followed me to the ends of the earth.

Writing coaches and teachers, starting with my fifth-grade teacher,
Richard Ward, who told me I was a good writer. My friend, **Bruce
Gelfand**, who coached and encouraged me for many years. And
Diana Loomans and **Karen Oxrider**, with whom I regularly
rendezvoused to write (and share my love of alliteration).

My family of origin and family of friends, especially
Dr. James Mellon and everyone at the **Global Truth
Center** who love and know the truth for me.

Everyone at **Advantage Media Group**, for encouraging
me and helping me to (finally!) finish this book.

And my beloved black kitties: **Petey, Littles, BooBoo,** and **Stinky**
who often cuddled next to me as I labored on my book …

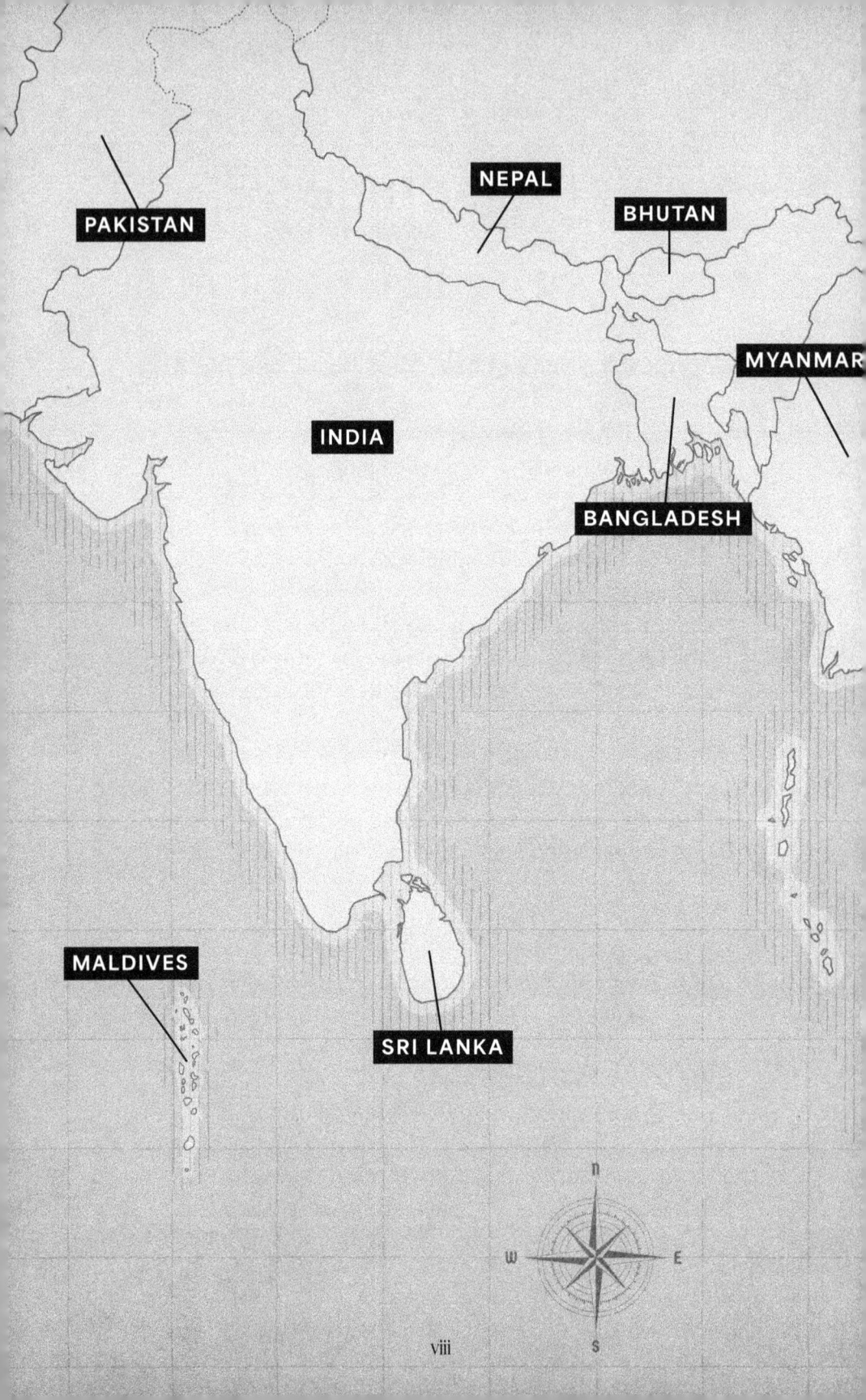

PAKISTAN

NEPAL

BHUTAN

MYANMAR

INDIA

BANGLADESH

MALDIVES

SRI LANKA

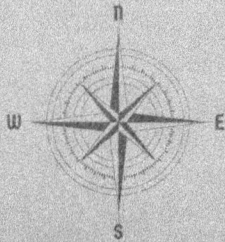

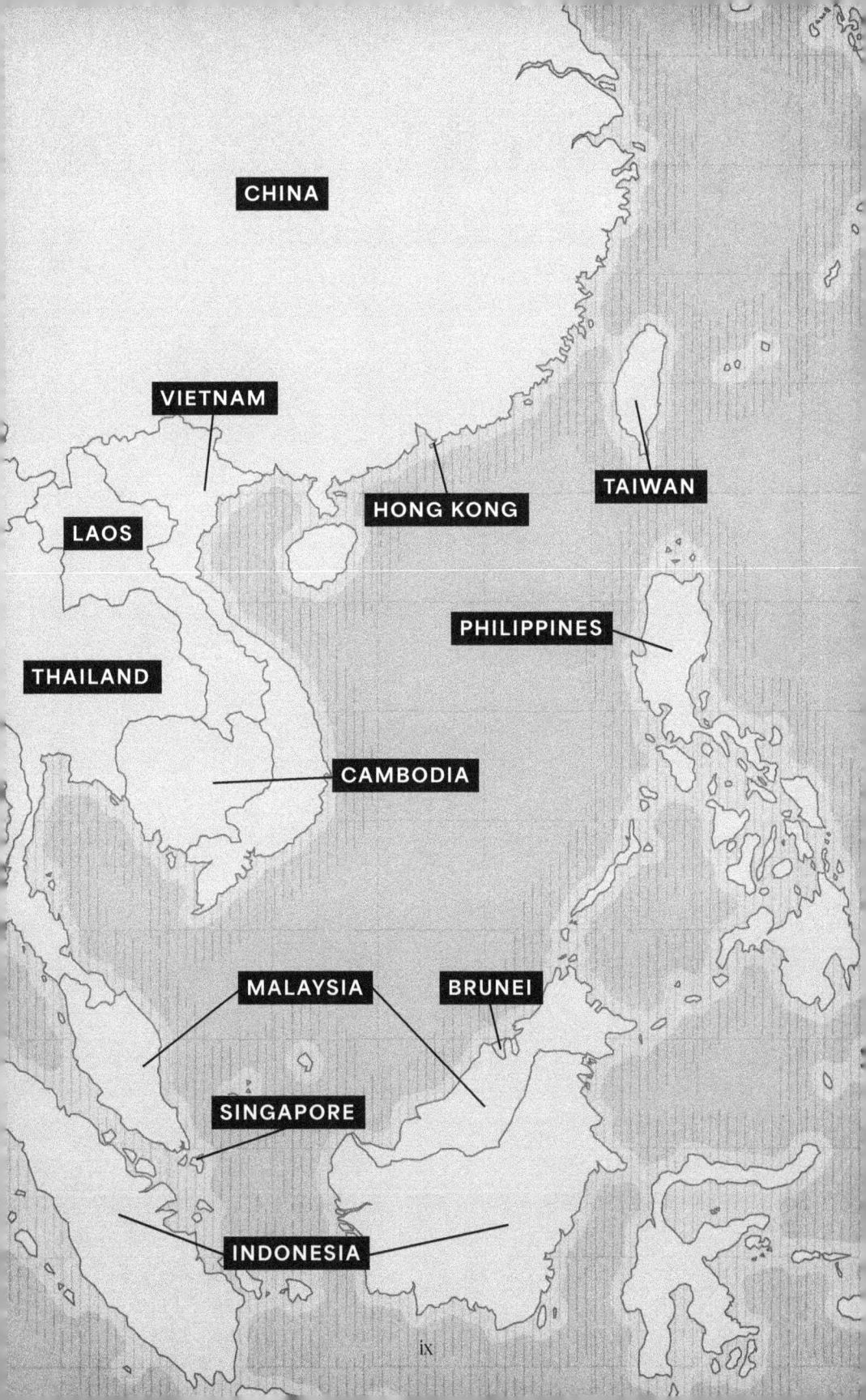

CHINA

VIETNAM

LAOS

THAILAND

HONG KONG

TAIWAN

PHILIPPINES

CAMBODIA

MALAYSIA

BRUNEI

SINGAPORE

INDONESIA

Preface

"Traveling – it leaves you speechless, then turns you into a storyteller."

—Ibn Battuta

This quote resonates with me because, with the publication of this book, I've become a storyteller.

But who the heck is Ibn Battuta? A quick search reveals that he was from a Berber tribe in North Africa, and he traveled the world way back in the 1300s. Near the end of his life, he dictated an account of his journeys, titled *A Gift to Those Who Contemplate the Wonders of Cities and the Marvels of Traveling*.

Like Ibn Battuta, I'm sharing my story to inspire you to seriously contemplate the marvels of traveling. (I'm *not* near the end of my life, by the way…)

My journey took eight months and occurred more than forty-five years ago—when the world wasn't digitized, suitcases didn't have wheels, and transactions were made with cash. It was a long time ago.

And the impact of that journey has lasted a lifetime.

This memoir took more than ten years to publish. The writing itself took a fraction of that time, but it took many years to define what I wanted to say. As often happens in life, stuff got in the way.

Like in 2016, when I was diagnosed with Stage 4 cancer which created a different priority: survival. But that's another memoir for another time.

Or, like in 2020, when COVID effectively shut down the world.

But here it is: my story of growing up. In 1978, I was twenty-three and adrift. I had graduated from Western Michigan University with a degree in Home Ec Education at a time when such subjects were being purged from high school curriculums. With no job prospects and no boyfriend, my only choice was to move back home to live with my parents in Saginaw, Michigan. A place to which I had sworn I would never return.

I spent many miserable months questioning every decision I'd ever made and wondering if I'd ever find fulfillment. And then one day, I received an airgram from my girlfriend, suggesting that I meet her in the Philippines when she finished her Peace Corps assignment. "We can travel together through southeast Asia and India," she wrote.

Finally, the lifeline I'd been waiting for!

As you'll read, the journey didn't go as planned. And, as often happens, the imperfection was absolutely perfect. What *did* happen catapulted me in a direction I never would have considered...and provided a foundation that served me personally, professionally, and spiritually for the rest of my adult life.

My intention in sharing my story is to stir up that part of you that yearns to take a risk, to have an adventure, to break away from the comfort and security of your life. I hope you'll be inspired to travel more deeply and differently than you ever dreamed possible—to discover the treasures of this big, beautiful planet and, in the process, to discover the treasure within yourself.

Yes, there are considerations: Time and money are obvious challenges. Plus, "Who will I go with?" "I couldn't possibly do that!" "I'll do that when I'm older..."

The list is endless.

All I can say is—*Do it anyway*. I promise one thing: you'll never regret it.

It starts when you say yes.

P.S. These are personal impressions—captured in the form of diary entries—of a naïve twenty-something, and they do not necessarily provide an accurate historical or cultural context of the places mentioned.

September 5, 1978: Departure Day

This will be my second time on an airplane. My first flight—when I was thirteen—was unforgettable, in a not-good way.

That summer, I had spent several weeks in Virginia with my favorite cousin, Karen, while her Navy officer husband was deployed in the Mediterranean. She was like the big sister I never had, and I, as an infant and toddler, was the baby sister she always wanted. She doted and fussed over me like nobody else ever did.

Karen had been visiting her folks in Lansing with her three over-active young sons and invited me to join her on the drive back to Virginia Beach in her Winnebago motorhome. And then I would fly home later in the summer on the first airplane flight of my life. I jumped at the chance!

I had high expectations for my summer at the beach: a bikini body, flirtatious surfer boys, and a little adolescent mischief. But the reality was quite different—chubby thighs, suburbia, and sunburn. Karen lived miles from the beach and her three sons—the terrible trio—were rowdy and unmanageable. Still, it was more interesting than my summer in Saginaw would have been.

One evening, the phone rang as I was washing the dinner dishes. It had been another hot, muggy day. The boys—as usual—had enjoyed playing three-on-one against me. I once thought their antics were cute, but after being with them for five weeks, their mischievousness frustrated me.

"Marilyn," Karen called to me, "telephone. It's your dad."

That was strange. Mom was always the one who called. If Dad were around, he'd get on the line for a quick hello and a short chat about the Detroit Tigers. Otherwise, we didn't have much to talk about.

Drying my hands on the dish towel, Karen handed me the receiver from the wall-mounted phone, and I noticed a pained look on her face. I absently coiled the mustard-colored cord around my index finger. "Hi, Dad."

"Hi, honey. How are you?"

"I'm good."

"Are you having fun? Are the boys behaving?"

"Yeah, it's fun. A lot hotter here. I went to the beach yesterday. And the boys, well, sometimes they're good. And lots of times they're not."

"Yes, well…" he paused. I could hear him take a deep breath. "I wanted to let you know that your mother is in the hospital. She had surgery."

"Why? What for?" I stammered.

"She had a mastectomy."

I'd never heard that word before. "What's that?"

All I heard of his response were two words: *breast cancer*. I dropped the receiver to the floor and ran to my bedroom in tears. *No, no, no! This can't be happening!*

My mother had never been optimistic. She put on a front for the neighbors, or when we went to church, but in the privacy of our

4

day-to-day life at 1375 Glendale Street in Saginaw, she was always depressed—which nobody noticed more than me. Dad would go off to work, and my three brothers were busy playing sports. I was the only girl, so I had to help her with cleaning, hanging laundry and kitchen chores. I did my best to never upset her.

And now...?

I had been excited about my very first airplane flight—to be traveling so fast, so high. Now, I was afraid of what I was flying home to—a place that would certainly be even more depressing than when I left it.

Karen had taken me shopping for something special to wear for my flight home. As a mother of three boys, she was excited to dress me up. I didn't have the heart to tell her that I hated the ruffled pink dress she picked out. And with a new hairstyle and sparkly pink barrette, I felt more dorky than pretty.

Mom and Aunt Lil were waiting when my flight landed at Tri-City Airport in Saginaw. Mom looked pale, and I hugged her awkwardly, afraid of hurting her. She asked me to pose for a photo on the tarmac with the United airplane in the background. My smile was forced, barely concealing my dread.

Walking into the little yellow Cape Cod house my dad and uncles had built after the war felt like walking into a morgue. Something had sucked the life out of it. A table in the entryway was piled high with gifts from the previous night's party in celebration of my parent's twenty-fifth wedding anniversary. In the best of times, silver serving trays and bud vases were inappropriate for our family's modest lifestyle. But given that my mother had just had her right breast dug out of her chest a week ago, it all seemed especially wrong.

So, it's almost exactly ten years later and I'm at the same airport saying tearful goodbyes. My "noble experiment" of adventure has begun. As much as I dislike this place and am excited to get away, I love my family and friends and will miss them.

I packed and dressed carefully for this, my first international flight. My brand-new suitcase—navy canvas with brown vinyl trim and a matching shoulder tote—is packed full of polyesters that won't wrinkle, just as the travel experts suggested.

Connecting in Denver, I splurge $1.50 for a copy of *Cosmopolitan*. I've never related to articles in magazines like this, but I'm feeling like I might have new and exciting opportunities for romance. Maybe even sex! On the cover, I see the gorgeous face of Cristina Ferrare, fashion model, TV host, and wife of John DeLorean. Inside is a story titled "What Celebrities Do to Make Themselves Feel Better When They Are Low." I have no empathy. How difficult can it be to be a celebrity? I'm feeling stupid for wasting that $1.50.

Arriving in San Francisco just after noon, I'm relieved to see my suitcase on the baggage carousel, but there are no luggage carts anywhere around. As I lug my bags to the international terminal, I'm telling myself with every step, *I over-packed.* And my new shoes—cute as they are—are proving to be a mistake.

The Philippine Airlines counter is jammed, and I learn that the flight to Manila is delayed until 6 a.m. tomorrow. I tell myself, *Get used to it, Marilyn. This is just the beginning.*

Taking a seat nearby, I watch the chaos unfold as arriving passengers learn of the flight delay. One old Filipina is particularly entertaining, as she wanders around talking loudly to herself. After about an hour, I check back at the counter to learn that they have arranged complimentary hotel accommodations, but they've not announced it.

This rookie traveler thought I'd have to spend the night on an airport bench. Instead, I get a voucher for the Hyatt Hotel. Wow! I've never stayed at such a nice hotel before. And they gave me a meal voucher, too, so I order a shrimp dinner from room service. Another first!

September 6: SFO to Manila

The hotel operator calls at 3:45 a.m., as I requested. I shower, change, and put on my face. Back at the airport, I check in without incident.

It's really happening! I'm leaving today on a jet plane!

My seatmate is a native Filipino who hasn't been back to his home country in fifty years. Another guy, Val, is annoyingly flirtatious. Some Filipino ladies I befriended during yesterday's lengthy wait think we look cute together.

Ugh! I'm not interested in men. Certainly not now, on the cusp of the biggest adventure of my life.

It's about six hours until our refueling stop in Honolulu and another thirteen hours after that. I sleep a bit, but it's not a very comfortable seat. Once again, I tell myself, *Get used to it, Marilyn!*

Thinking ahead to the reunion with Barbara, I wonder how she'll have changed. She has a new best friend—another Peace Corps volunteer named Harriet. They've shared some incredible experiences together, so I couldn't possibly object when I learned that she, too, would be traveling with us. No doubt I'll be the third wheel. I just hope Barbara still likes me.

September 8

The flight lands in Manila in the middle of the afternoon, but it's midnight by my body clock. Plus, we've crossed the International

Date Line, so I'm completely disoriented. The crush of people pushing and shoving at the airport is as oppressive as the heat and humidity. Everyone is speaking all at once in sing-song voices, and I can't understand a damn thing. My blistered feet are killing me. Val tries to be helpful, and I just want him to leave me alone! It takes forever, but my luggage eventually arrives, and I frantically begin my search for Barbara. Finally, I see her waving at me from the sidewalk outside the terminal. I push through the teeming crowd toward her outstretched arms. It's an emotional reunion, with hugs and lots of tears.

Standing nearby, Harriet is a tall, curly-haired redhead from Montana. Her hug is warm and welcoming, so my first impression is a good one.

Cabbies and vendors vie for our attention, honking and hollering. I'm completely overwhelmed. I guess this is culture shock? Or jet lag—or both?

We climb into a taxi, and Barbara instructs the driver to take us to Santos, the small hotel where all Peace Corps volunteers stay when they come to Manila. As I expected, it's nothing fancy. My room has a sink, toilet, and open shower.

We imbibe White Russians as we talk and talk and talk through the evening. Barbara is just as I remember her: energetic, gracious, and receptive. She always makes me feel special.

I'm happy that she's happy that I'm here.

♀ ———— ♀

September days in Manila…

Everything is new and foreign. I'm tired, scared, and intimidated by just about everything. Traffic is chaotic. Food is very eclectic and exotic. I'm trying to gradually assimilate to the cuisine, but I know I can't baby myself forever. I taste Indian curry for the first time, as well as squid, quail eggs, and mango.

My mattress is lumpy and the pillow even lumpier. I yearn for the down-filled pillow of home. I don't sleep well and wake up at ungodly hours for the first several nights here. My thoughts are more negative and scared than excited. This is not how I expected to feel.

I'm introduced to lots of Peace Corps volunteers, all of whom who pepper me with questions about what's going on back in the States. I grope for answers that hopefully make me sound intelligent and knowledgeable, but I'm realizing just how ill-informed I am—and how I've taken my rights and privileges as an American for granted.

It'll be a few more weeks before we depart from the Philippines, so Barbara recommends that I book a package tour to Hong Kong. It's gonna cost over $200 for airfare and hotel for seven nights. Barbara knows two girls who will be on the tour, and I'm hopeful I can hang with them or find another traveler to pair up with. Gotta psych myself up for traveling independently.

We discuss our future travel plans, and I'm pleased that we are all on the same page: Singapore, Malaysia, Thailand, and India. I sure hope my money holds out.

Monday, September 11: Cebu

I've traveled with Barbara to the southern island of Cebu to visit Tony and Chris, where I get my first glimpse of rural Filipino life. I smell open fires, tropical flowers, and fresh sea air. I travel on a gaudily painted jeepney crowded with people of all ages, passing open-air markets teeming with activity as American rock-and-roll music blares away on the tape deck. There are no frills, which seems at first to be due to poverty—but I've been noticing that people don't seem impoverished. They don't have anything to compare it to. Everyone stares, but most respond to a smile with a smile of their own.

Driving to the beach, we pass through lush greenery of banana, coconut, and mango trees. Houses are crude and simple, constructed of wood, bamboo, and thatch—often built on stilts to avoid damage from flooding and rodents. Windows are open to allow for ventilation and natural light.

Visiting a leprosarium where they weave bamboo baskets, I spend tons of money on their beautiful products. And I have the privilege of meeting Sister Germaine, the closest thing to a saint that I've ever encountered.

Friday, September 15: Cebu to Manila

Barbara and I arrive back in Manila laden with eight pieces of baggage from all our purchases in Cebu. We are at the mercy of unscrupulous porters and taxi drivers who see two vulnerable young women and have no compunction about taking full advantage of our helplessness. I am nervous and frightened, trying to keep an eye on all our stuff while Barbara shouts and swears at taxi drivers who want to charge three times what a ride should cost. Finally, we pile into a car which barely accommodates us and our baggage, figuring we'll short-change him when he drops us off. But he stops at a gas station en route and won't move until we pay for his gas!

Later that afternoon, I realize my purse has been slashed. Fortunately, they took only a cosmetic pouch, not any money or—god forbid!—my passport. But we are safely back at Santos, and I have learned a lesson: to be mindful of my surroundings and less vulnerable in my future travels.

Marilyn, you're definitely not in Saginaw anymore.

September 28

I wake up early and call home—collect—before 8 a.m. As usual, everything's fine, nothing has changed, except that Mom informs me—to my great surprise—that she's gone out and gotten a job! For years, I'd encouraged her to find something to do besides housework, to improve her self-confidence and meet people outside of the neighborhood and church community. It's a mindless job—inserting advertising supplements into the Sunday Saginaw News. But it's something. I'm proud of her—and tell her so. Barbara postulates that she's probably done it to take her mind off of worrying about me. Whatever her reason, the news makes my day.

Assorted observations...

I'm amazed at the inefficiency of this place. It takes at least ten tries to make a phone call. I'm charged an extra two pesos for a spoonful of chocolate syrup in a chocolate soda. The flight we took to Cebu in the southern Philippines was only an hour, but the return by ferry was twenty-four hours.

I've attracted lots of attention from men—both Filipino and American. At first, I found it very flattering, but eventually decided that I'm a novelty—a fresh face—and they're just testing the waters of the new girl in town.

One evening after dinner, I walk with a Peace Corps volunteer through Rizal Park, named after the Filipino patriot, José Rizal, whose execution fanned the flames of revolution against the kingdom of Spain in the late 1800s. I am shocked to see dozens and dozens of people sleeping on concrete benches—with no pillows or blankets. If they dare to change positions in their sleep, they'll certainly fall onto the sidewalk. I am fascinated and wish I had a camera to record the wide variety of ages and creative sleeping positions. Afterward, we have ice cream at a cafe run by the deaf.

Tuesday, October 3: Manila to Sablayan

Sablayan is a coastal village on the island of Mindoro. Barbara had arrived here two years ago with another volunteer, at which time they were told by Mrs. Babia, the bank manager, to "implement a municipal nutrition program."

That was all. They got no guidance, no suggested first steps, no local connections, no specific instructions from the Peace Corps. They were a couple of twenty-two-year-old American social work majors who had *no* idea what they were doing.

Besides Mrs. Babia, nobody in Sablayan spoke English except for the smarmy partner of the female doctor with whom Barbara lived for her first year. But Barbara was motivated and disciplined to learn Tagalog, the local language, so she could effectively communicate with the residents.

She lives in a two-bedroom nipa hut on the shore of the South China Sea. It has a thatched roof, bamboo floors, wood siding and contains a table, chairs, and a two-burner camp stove. Sometimes, she has electricity for as many as three hours a day. She hired the boy next door to deliver water for her toilet every day. Two hammocks hang on the deck, where she spends the majority of her leisure time.

Like everyone in the town, she goes to the market every day since she has no refrigeration. She eats dried fish and rice daily. During the months-long rainy season, Barbara's house never dries out.

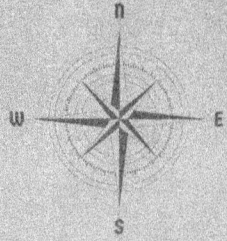

Wednesday, October 4

Today is the day that Barbara is buying Linda's freedom. Linda is the housekeeper for the town's female doctor and her dubious live-in partner. Linda is a beautiful, illiterate, naïve nineteen-year-old who is the sole support for two lazy parents and several siblings. Her parents are indebted to Doctora for 300 pesos (about $40). Linda yearns to be liberated from this form of indentured servitude and the roving hands of the doctor's boyfriend, but her parents depend on her income.

Barbara has arranged for Linda to be employed as a housekeeper for a Peace Corps administrator in Manila. There, she will have an opportunity for a fresh start at a better life.

Wow. *This is the kind of stuff I read about—but it's happening here in real life!*

Friday, October 6

This is my best day in Sablayan. Alan, one of Barbara's Filipino friends, and Georgette, a Peace Corps volunteer from a nearby village, accompany me to see the farms of the San Sebastian school. The rice paddies are beautiful, and it's great to walk around them—until I manage to fall in. Alan climbs a coconut tree to cut down some young fruit and his parents feed us a lunch that is *masarap* (delicious), featuring freshly harvested rice like I've never tasted before.

We meet the squatters on their land, Negritas—a dark-skinned minority tribe of African descent—who peddle their natural herbal medicines in town. The young mother wears her blouse unbuttoned so that her baby can nurse whenever she wants. They all smoke hand-rolled cigarettes—even a little girl who looks to be about six years old.

Once again, I pinch myself. *Marilyn, you're a long, long way from Saginaw, Michigan.*

Sunday, October 8: Departing Sablayan

We do our final packing in the light of dawn. Even at this early hour, Barbara's house is filled with people. The emotion is palpable. Barbara sobs as the jeep pulls away from her little nipa hut.

At the dock, dozens of people have come to see her off. A banca (boat) has been hired to take us up the coast to the town of Mamburao, from where we'll take a short flight to Manila. Otherwise, traveling by passenger ship would take us eighteen hours. But, typical of this place, the boat doesn't leave on time—even though it is privately hired. Barbara has pulled it together and is smiling and joyous. Linda, who is leaving the only place she's ever known, looks numb. And I don't know what to say or do.

Finally, it's time to go. I hug her best friends—Manny, Alan, Emmy, and Efren, with whom Barbara has had a romantic relationship. I barely know these people, but my eyes are filled with tears. Meanwhile, Barbara is laughing, smiling, and waving a red kerchief as the banca pulls away from the dock and slowly makes its way upriver.

"I want them to remember me as happy," she tells me.

Her self-control is amazing.

It's been such a fascinating experience to come here and meet these people whose lives are so fundamentally different from mine. Most of the young people here will never leave Sablayan, not even to go to Manila. There's not much opportunity for anyone.

Reminds me a little of Saginaw.

Monday, October 16: Back in Manila

We were scheduled to leave the country today. But we're going nowhere.

Apparently, the United States government is out of business. October 1 begins a new fiscal year, and all funding decisions were supposed to be in place on that date. But President Carter vetoed some Congressional funding bills, so the government has effectively shut down. And departing Peace Corps volunteers, who are supposed to receive money to buy plane tickets out of here, are going nowhere.

So, we're stuck here for who knows how long. I'm sick of Manila, sick of the Peace Corps clique with all their stories, sick of the food, the heat and humidity, the traffic—just sick of all of it. I'm beginning to think that this trip was a big mistake. It certainly has not been anything like I imagined. I can't wait till we're all on the road together, on equal footing.

I'm lonely. Barbara is so buddy-buddy with Harriet, and she seems distant these days, so, I don't feel comfortable confiding in her. I'm bored. I've seen the major sights—such as they are in this hellhole of a city. I loved visiting Barbara's village of Sablayan. And I had a pleasant few days in the mountainous resort of Baguio. I loved my weeklong package tour to Hong Kong, but I spent lots of money on souvenirs and stuff that necessitated spending lots *more* money to ship it all back home.

Today was the day the three of us—Barbara, Harriet, and myself—were supposed to fly to a place called Kota Kinabalu on the island of Sabah, which is part of Malaysia. The Lonely Planet guidebook has nothing particularly good to say about Kota Kinabalu, which was destroyed in World War II, but Harriet has the hots for an ex-volunteer who lives there. Apparently, he gets paid to collect tropical fish for export. Now, there's a profession I never would have considered! But those colorful fish have to come from somewhere, right?

After that, our Malaysian Airways routing includes a flight to Singapore. And the third and final segment is to Kuala Lumpur, the capital of Malaysia. But we cannot leave the Philippines until Barbara and Harriet get their payout from the Peace Corps. And nobody can predict when that will happen.

During dinner tonight, a couple of volunteers named Dan and Adam mention that they're heading up to Baguio in the morning. I must be emboldened by the White Russian cocktails I'm drinking, as I make an audacious move and invite myself along on their getaway.

I've got to get out of here!

Tuesday, October 17: To Baguio

Our bus leaves mid-afternoon and not a minute too soon for me. The bus station is pure madness—crowded and hot, with everyone pushing and shoving. I even saw people crawling through windows. Luckily, our bus is only half full.

It's such a relief to be out of Manila and into the countryside, where I witness a breathtaking sight. A water-filled rice paddy reflects the blazing golden sky as a farmer leads a string of four caribou, juxtaposed against the blinding bright gold with rice terraces and seedlings adding design and texture. In the background, the mountains shield the sun as it leaves this day, leaving me with a never-to-be-forgotten moment of beauty.

And to think that if I'd left the country yesterday as originally planned, I'd have missed this experience! Perhaps this is the sign of hope I've been looking for. I resolve to be more aware, cherishing these emotions and observations—and etching them into memory.

Baguio calls itself "the City of Pines" and is famous for its green park spaces and hillsides teeming with gigantic pine trees. It's much cooler than Manila. Already I'm feeling rejuvenated and much happier. Dan and Adam are great companions, and the dinner I enjoy at Camp John Hay, the US Air Force base, is absolutely scrumptious—

a succulent steak paired with a perfectly baked potato. It's been a long time since I ate something so familiar.

After dinner, we watch some American television: *The Love Boat!*

Wednesday, October 18: Baguio

For the past few months, Baguio has hosted the prestigious World Chess Championship, featuring an intense face-off between two Russian grandmasters, Korchnoi and Karpov. I recall reading about this matchup last summer in a *Saginaw News* story. Perhaps chess champions are all a bit eccentric, but these two guys take it to another level, attracting headlines with outlandish accusations of secret codes hidden in a delivery of blueberry yogurt, alleged hypnotism, and other bizarre incidents.

Their thirty-second—and final—chess match concluded today, with Karpov emerging triumphant. How unimaginable for me to be here—all the way from Saginaw, Michigan—witnessing this historic day first-hand.

Also unimaginable is my introduction to two of Korchnoi's spiritual teachers from the Ananda Marga sect. They are dressed in orange-and-white guru-type outfits and are as interesting to look at as they are to listen to. They speak eloquently and intelligently about their religion, which combines spiritualism with service to humanity. It all sounds pretty sensible to me, and they're not the starry-eyed dreamers most yogis seem to be. Later, we all go down to the stream where they meditate, as I just sit and ponder my thoughts.

I feel as if I've not grown or changed since I left home six weeks ago, and I resolve to change that. I've been judgmental and self-absorbed. Just as yesterday's beautiful sunset scene of the rice paddy made clear, I should check in with myself more often and be grateful for this incredible opportunity to see the world.

Thursday, October 19: Baguio

Late this morning, Adam and I walk to the park to commune with nature for a while. Then to a Daoist Temple where they have a ritual of telling fortunes with incense and shaking a stick from a bamboo container after you've posed a question or problem to the gods. My first question is, "Will I achieve—within the near future—my goal of self-confidence and independence?"

The answer: "Do not hurry. Everything will come in due time."

Hmmm. Seems a bit vague, but at least they didn't say no!

Friday, October 20: Baguio

The day unfolds in all its beauty, but I must depart today. With a hint of amusement, I step aboard the 9 a.m. "Victory Liner" (a rather fancy name for a bus) bound for Manila. I'm optimistic that we'll leave the country on Monday and must purchase our tickets today. I'm feeling good—more spiritual and in the right frame of mind to cope with whatever lies ahead.

But my positivity lasts only until the city limits of Manila—dirty, congested, and polluted. Upon arriving at Santos, I receive the disheartening news that the expected government money has *not* come through. A wave of depression engulfs me, and a sense of hopelessness and helplessness takes hold.

The following days pass by in a blur—I'm feeling listless, restless, and overwhelmed with homesickness. In the middle of the night, I awaken to excruciating pain in my eyes, as if they're filled with grit. Rinsing with water doesn't help to alleviate the discomfort. I lie motionless in bed, trying not to move my eyeballs, but the pain is still unbearable.

On top of it, Barbara is very sick—fever, vomiting, chills, diarrhea, and blood in her stool. We take her to the hospital, where she's admitted.

As long as I'm there, I see a doctor about my eyes. His diagnosis: a cold is causing blockage of my tear ducts. I'm relieved to have a diagnosis, and they're already starting to feel a bit better.

Meanwhile, Harriet is driving everyone crazy. She's playing mother hen to Barbara and won't let anyone interfere.

But the three of us have reached an agreement on one thing. I'm going to fly out ahead of them, and they'll catch up after the government funds are released and when Barbara is healthy again. Harriet seems anxious to see me go. I can't shake this lingering feeling that she'll manipulate everything to ensure we never truly connect.

Wednesday, October 25: Departure Eve

Today is my last day in the Philippines. Finally, I'm getting out of this place. I'm excited and nervous. I'll be flying to a place I've never heard of—Kota Kinabalu—and staying with a guy I've never met. Traveling solo. This is so unlike anything I've ever done before, but everything about this trip—so far—is unlike anything I've ever done before.

Barbara is still hospitalized—but getting better. I visited her this morning, intending to confide my fear that Harriet will sabotage our plans to travel together. But before I say anything, Barbara speaks up. "It'll be so great when we finally get on the road together."

So, I decide to keep my negative opinion to myself. I don't like being so judgmental and cynical about Harriet. It's not fair. But in truth, I'm jealous of her tight friendship with Barbara. I find it interesting that both of them insist they are independent women, but they depend on each other in so many ways.

Tonight, to my surprise, Harriet presents me with a cake for my birthday (which is in two days) during my going-away dinner. I can't help but feel guilty for doubting her sincerity earlier, and I genuinely hope that she's doing it out of kindness.

Thursday, October 26: I'm Off!

Distances are deceptive here in the south Pacific; the flight to Kota Kinabalu is almost six hours long. This place was Harriet's choice, since she has a crush on Mike, a former volunteer with the Peace Corps.

KK, as they call it, is a relatively modern town, having been totally rebuilt after the war. The architecture is a mix of Chinese, Malay, and Middle Eastern. The island is called Sabah, which means "the land below the winds." They don't get typhoons here. The trees are beautiful, and there's a great selection of vegetables in the market. But it's expensive here, so I'm glad my lodging is free.

Friday, October 27: Kota Kinabalu

This is a very different birthday. I saved the birthday cards I received from my parents and two of my brothers and read them all today— between tears of homesickness.

I'm reading a very enlightening book: *Passages,* which I bought at the bookstore at the Manila airport. It's about the "predictable crises of adult life." The author, Gail Sheehy, writes about the conflict of leaving home, security, and safety to establish oneself as a separate entity, with all the risk and hardship it entails. According to her theory, this trip for me is a moratorium—a way of putting off the crisis for a while.

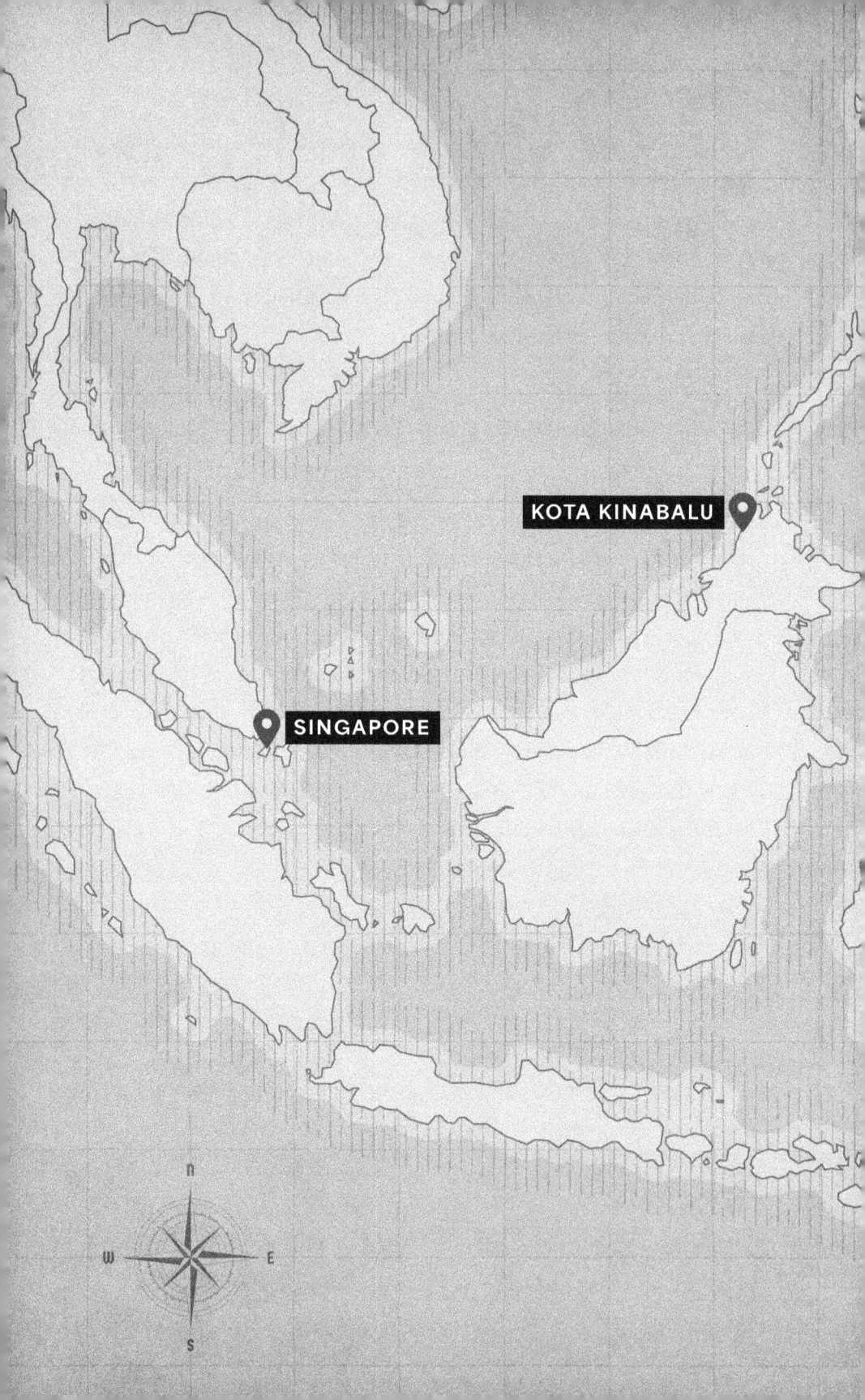

KOTA KINABALU

SINGAPORE

Although it doesn't seem as if my crisis has been put off, I feel like I'm living it! Most everything that could go wrong with our plan to travel together has gone wrong. Among other things, each of us has changed. Or, more accurately, Barbara has evolved and grown even more confident and assertive while I've just stagnated. Her personal transformation is amazing, and oh, how I envy her.

Mike has been a gracious host. He took me to dinner at the Kinabalu International Hotel to celebrate my birthday, where we met a wacky old Australian couple at the bar. She just loves us "Yanks" and was the mood-brightener I need right now.

Sunday, October 29: Kota Kinabalu

I'm frustrated because there's no way to know when Barbara and Harriet might arrive here. Communication just isn't possible—phone calls are much too expensive. Obviously, the adventure I had envisioned is not happening. What should I do? Seems as if I have only two choices: go on alone or go home. I lack the courage and confidence to travel solo. Nor can I bear the thought of surrendering and returning home to my boring life.

I think back to the Daoist Temple I visited in Baguio, when the spiritual answer to my question was, "Do not hurry. Everything will come in due time." So, I've decided not to decide. At least for today.

But am I being spiritual, or am I just a chicken and avoiding the obvious?

I don't know. I'll decide tomorrow. Or maybe the next day.

Monday, October 30: Arrive Singapore

I finally decided. I've moved on to Singapore. Whether this is the end of the road for me or not...I'll decide later.

Singapore is a big city. It's an island, and it's a country, too.

And it's efficient, as I breeze through Customs and Immigration at the airport and easily find bus 91, which will drop me close to the hotel where I hope to stay. I admire the beautiful landscaping, modern skyscrapers, and wide, tidy streets. Laws are very strict. Littering is a crime! Smoking is prohibited in public places. And they don't like hippies—apparently, guys with long hair can be turned away at the border.

Water is drinkable from the tap.

Ah, yes. I think I'm gonna like it here!

On the flight over, I read about Singapore in my guidebook. In 1819, Sir Stamford Raffles "claimed" this quiet fishing village for the British Empire, which subsequently established major military and naval bases here. In the late 1950s, Singapore became a self-governing nation. It enjoys a very strategic location—at the tip of the Malay Peninsula, flanked by the Pacific and Indian Oceans—and is one of Asia's most important seaports.

Compared to the Philippines, Singapore is modern and prosperous. Traffic flows smoothly. Buses run on schedule. Motorists even yield to pedestrians instead of trying to run them down!

The bus drops me a couple of blocks from the Tong Ah Hotel, which is highly recommended in my Lonely Planet guidebook. Somehow, I manage to carry my heavy suitcase and shoulder tote without my arms falling off. The hotel is full, but I'm put on a waitlist and will check back tomorrow.

At a different hotel a few blocks away, I meet a Malaysian guy who is also looking for a cheap, single room. We're told there are no singles, but there is a double available. His name is Ton—or maybe he said Tom, but I'm embarrassed to ask him to repeat himself. He proposes that we share the double, and I agree—as long as there are two beds.

Whew! This will be the first time in my life that I'm sharing a bedroom with a boy! Being the only girl in my family, I never even had to share a bedroom with a sister. This guy is a perfect stranger, but my intuition tells me he's harmless. I hope so!

The room is adequate, and there are, indeed, two beds. The bathroom is down the hall—with a squat toilet. *Good for the thighs,* I think to myself.

Ton (or Tom) and I go out looking for something to eat and happen upon—of all places—"Colonel Sanders." Seems as if they've dropped any reference to "Kentucky" since people here wouldn't know what that is.

"Let's eat here," he suggests.

I can't help but notice how greasy it is! And expensive. But he picks up the dinner tab, which I appreciate. I struggle to keep a conversation going, and am less nervous about sharing a room with this timid guy...I'm pretty sure I won't be fighting him off tonight.

I'm feeling happy, which feels strange. I guess it's been a while. There's no question that things haven't worked out, but I'm adapting and making decisions that so far *have* worked out. Maybe this is the way it's gonna be from now on. *Maybe I've got more spunk than I thunk!*

Tuesday, October 31

My intuition about Ton was accurate. I got a good night's sleep.

Hungry for comfort food, I seek out the Song Heng Wee restaurant, which, according to Lonely Planet, has the best toast and marmalade in town.

Later in the day, I check back at the Tong Ah and discover there is a single room opening up. I pack up my things, say goodbye to Ton, and schlep my too-heavy suitcase the few blocks back to Beach Road, vowing with every step to lighten my load.

Settling into my tiny room, I wonder what my friends will be doing back at home on this Halloween night. Probably meeting up at the Green Hut bar in Bay City to get wasted.

My happiness from yesterday is wearing thin. I look for a place to get my hair cut and permed, without success. My shoe falls apart and, while waiting for it to get repaired, I order soup from a food stall and can't eat it—too spicy. I get back to my room late in the afternoon with a splitting headache. I crawl into bed and read a few more pages of *Passages*, which is providing me with lots of insight. No surprise that I'm in the midst of my "Trying Twenties"—basically trying to figure out what I want from life.

The case histories in the chapter about love provide evidence that romantic love isn't enough for a successful marriage. Partners who emphasize friendship and cooperation have better relationships than those who rely on love to keep it together. I wonder if I'll ever wean myself away from my idealized vision of love. The psychology seems plausible and more realistic—sharing my life with someone with whom I feel a close camaraderie instead of with some guy who sweeps me off my feet. But so far, at least, I haven't had either experience.

Frankly, I don't know what I want. I just want Barbara to show up so this trip can start happening like it's supposed to.

Wednesday, November 1

Singapore is my favorite place so far. I can't believe how such a big city can be so clean and orderly. I learn that family planning is strongly encouraged—families with more than two kids pay extra taxes. In the very heart of the city, cars are not allowed unless they have at least four persons inside—to encourage carpooling and cut down on traffic congestion and pollution. This country has *really* got it together!

There are many American sailors here, enjoying a few days of "liberty" while their ship is in port. Maybe it's a sailor thing, but they are *so* obnoxious! I'm embarrassed that they're Americans—and just a bunch of drunken fools. They've probably been on board ship for so long that they've forgotten how to act on land!

I'm staying healthy…trying to eat sensibly, taking my vitamins, and using water purification tablets—even though Singapore's tap water is supposedly safe. I swear that I walk at least five miles a day, rarely using buses or taxis. I should have lost weight, but I don't feel much thinner. I haven't been on a scale since I left Manila.

I love the food here—especially from the plentiful and inexpensive hawker food stalls. Chinese food is certainly different than that of the Forbidden City restaurant in Saginaw. Lots spicier—but good. And then, there's Malay food—laksas and fish paste and coconut milk and banana leaves and sambal, which I've learned the hard way, is spicy chili paste. There are lots of Indian restaurants with fragrant curries which I'm too timid to try. But the fresh fruit stalls are my favorite. I've never had such delicious fruit! Mangoes, rambutan, jackfruit, and pineapple like I've never tasted before. Really, really good!

What a way to achieve my goal of self-reliance and independence. Of course, I've got a ways to go yet, but this is getting to be a real confidence-booster!

It's sunset, and I'm listening to evening prayers being chanted from the nearby Muslim mosque. The smell of incense is everywhere. Most of the older people dress traditionally, in sarongs. Men's are typically plain or plaid, while women's are batik prints. Indian women wear saris with their caste mark on their forehead. Chinese men wear baggy shorts, and women wear silk pajama outfits. The diversity is refreshing. It's all starting to look familiar.

I'm excited to see the famous Raffles Hotel nearby. A hundred years ago, Rudyard Kipling advised, "When in Singapore, put up at the Raffles." I can't afford to stay there, but at least I'll go inside and order a Singapore Sling—where they were invented!

Tuesday, November 7

The waiting and wondering is getting old. I'm feeling abandoned, frustrated, and lonely. Maybe this adventure just wasn't meant to be. I consider buying a ticket and surprising my family for the holidays. What a splendid homecoming that would be—for about a day. And then, I'd be as unhappy and unsettled as before.

Dammit! Where *are* Barbara and Harriet?

Meanwhile, here I am at a busy Singapore intersection, waiting on a traffic signal. A little Caucasian lady—shorter than me—is standing next to me. She's about my mother's age, and she's bouncing with energy. In my sour mood, I find her vitality annoying.

We exchange pleasantries. I'm grumpy, but I can't be rude.

From her accent, she's obviously British. For no good reason, this annoys me even more. The light turns green, and she strides across the street with a purposeful gait. I pick up my pace to keep up. More pleasantries are exchanged as we walk together for the next block, during which she reveals that she had, for her entire life, traveled with her husband.

"He died in April, but I know he would have wanted me to keep going." she explained.

We part ways at the next traffic signal—but the encounter has stayed with me. It's a random meeting, but the message is clear to me: *Stop the pity party and just keep going, Marilyn. And do it solo. And do it with guts and with gusto.*

Wednesday, November 8

I can't afford to stay at the Tong Ah any longer, so I decide to move to the Katong YMCA, which is only $4 per night. Many Vietnamese refugees are staying here. The change of scene is nice, and it's very quiet except when planes are approaching the airport. It's exciting to think of all the neat places they're coming from!

Reminds me of when I was a little girl—lying on the grass in my backyard, looking up at the vapor trails made by teeny, tiny airplanes slicing through the mid-Michigan clouds. *I wonder what it's like to fly so high?*, I would think. And, *Where are those people going?* And—something that was almost too improbable to consider—*I wonder if I'll ever fly on one of those airplanes?*

Which triggers another childhood memory, when we took a family vacation to Washington, DC, and my dad asked each of us kids in turn, "Where do you want to go while we're here?" My oldest brother, Jim—strait-laced and analytical—was destined to be an engineer. He announced: "I want to go to the Smithsonian Museum." Bob, a year and a half older than me, wanted to see the changing of the guard at the Tomb of the Unknown Soldier.

And then, it was my turn, and I gleefully exclaimed, "I want to go to the airport!"

It was the best part of that family vacation for me, as Dad parked our Chevy Impala station wagon on a frontage road near National Airport as giant planes zoomed down the runway and soared overhead into the wild blue yonder. Destined for exciting cities like San Francisco, or Paris, or possibly even Singapore!

The girl in charge here at the YMCA is very helpful. She finds a box for me so I can mail my impractical polyesters home. In the afternoon, I go to the Tong Ah with a letter for Barbara and Harriet to let them know where I'm staying, in the event that they ever actually arrive here.

But there's a telegram waiting for me: "Flights fully booked. School holidays. Will keep trying."

When I departed Manila two weeks ago, I'd been unaffected. But apparently the "open" ticket we bought, which gave us flexibility of travel dates, is a "space-available" ticket. I had no problem getting on a flight out of Manila, but Malaysian schools are now on holiday, and every seat is taken. It's anybody's guess how long they'll be stuck in Manila.

My reaction borders on amusement at this point. The delays are getting comical.

My Singapore visa is valid for only ten days, so I apply for an extension. I doubt that many people stay here longer than ten days—there's not that much to see and do.

I check out the bookstores to kill time. I find an interesting book about batik, but it's closing time, so I'll come back tomorrow to look at it further before deciding to buy or not. I go to the Satay Club for dinner and order *Mee Goreng*, a Malaysian specialty. It's spaghetti-type noodles with a spicy red sauce, stir-fried with vegetables, meat, and egg. Another goodie is Satay—chunks of meat (mostly beef or chicken) on small skewers, cooked over a charcoal fire and eaten with a spicy peanut sauce.

Nobody has checked into my dormitory-style room, so I've got some privacy to think. I've been on my own for two weeks and am functioning fairly well. I've never been alone like this—without friends or family around—for this long a period in my life. Perhaps, I'm more independent than I give myself credit for! Most likely, this is an introduction to the "aloneness" I'll undoubtedly feel if I move to Chicago or another big city as I'm hoping to do after finishing this trip. But after this, I think I can do it!

Sunday, November 12

Kerrie, from Australia, moved into my dorm room today. It's nice to finally have some company. I immediately envy her lean, lithe body and her confident, carefree outlook. It occurs to me that I've hardened over here—taking people too seriously and not finding the humor in various situations. I'm often moody and defensive. I'm struggling with mounting feelings of frustration because nothing is working out as I'd hoped.

On the one hand, I want to go home. It sounds so good. I feel as if I'm ready to face the challenge of finding a job. And it would be so much fun to surprise everyone by showing up in time for Christmas. I'm tired of living out of a suitcase and wearing the same shabby clothes that never really get clean in cold-water soakings.

On the other hand, I question whether I'm rationalizing myself out of a less-than-ideal life situation. It would be a huge cop-out to call it quits and run back home—right?

I flagellate constantly between one decision and the other, suspecting that I'll be sorry if I throw in the towel at this point.

So, every day I decide to give it another day.

Meanwhile, I've explored almost everything on Lonely Planet's list of, "Things to Do in Singapore." I've done Chinatown with its maze of stalls and streets with laundry hanging from every balcony. Thieves Market off Arab Street was fascinating the first and second time I went there. Lots of tempting things to buy, but anticipating the expense of shipping my purchases back home tempered the fun. Tiger Balm Gardens is as gaudy as the guidebook said it would be, but at least it's free. Orchid Gardens is beautiful—but boring. I've done the requisite harbor cruise. I chose not to visit the Alligator Farm after reading that the critters are destined to be handbags. And, of course, I've enjoyed Singapore Slings at Raffles on a few occasions when I've felt like splurging.

Wednesday, November 15: To Kuala Lumpur, Malaysia

That's it! I've finally made a decision.

I met a girl named Pat on Monday at the Newton Circus food stalls who, unknowingly, influenced my decision. She had been on the road for nearly eighteen months, the last six of which were solo. She'd started her trip with a boyfriend and eventually split off and went her own way. I had so many questions that I dared not ask: *How could she afford it? Did she work along the way? Did she like traveling solo? Did she ever get lonely?*

Once again, it seemed like fate (or whatever you call it) was sending a signal. If she could do it…why not me?

My flight leaves this afternoon. I'll use the last segment of my airline ticket to get to Kuala Lumpur and then I'll travel north up the Malaysian peninsula to Thailand and buy a cheap ticket home from Bangkok. I should still be able to surprise the family for Christmas.

I rush out to buy some Tiger Balm ointment and film, stopping at the Tong Ah to say goodbye to Woo and leave a note for Barbara and Harriet.

Thursday, November 16: Kuala Lumpur

It's not fair to compare places—but I much prefer Singapore. The drivers here in KL, as they call it, would rather hit you than yield to a pedestrian; few people seem to speak English; there's nothing tempting in the shops; and I'm frequently lost.

But I manage to find my way to the Peace Corps office where there are a few letters waiting—from Mom and my friend, Sheila. Mom's correspondence is touching, even a bit empathic—and

PENANG

KUALA LUMPUR

makes me glad I'll be home for Christmas. Sheila's letter is short and forcibly written—nothing much has changed with my gang of friends back home.

I'm staying at the YWCA, which is a permanent home for many working girls. I haven't been in the company of so many females since dormitory life at Western Michigan University!

A couple of Peace Corps volunteers who live here suggest that I take the night train to Penang tomorrow at 10 p.m. There's nothing keeping me here, so I make my way to the elaborate Moorish railway station and reserve a sleeping berth on tomorrow's train for 26 Malaysian ringgit (about US$12).

Saturday, November 18: Arrive Penang

It was a long night. The rocking motion, frequent stops, and "clackety-clack" noise of the overnight train were not conducive to sleep. Arriving at the rail station in Butterworth, Malaysia, I'm mobbed by porters offering to help with my suitcase. I wave them off, knowing the ferry terminal is within walking distance.

The two-minute walk, lugging my heavy suitcase and matching shoulder tote, reminds me how foolish I'd been with my preparations for this journey: Expecting my friendship with Barbara to pick up where it left off was unrealistic. And packing mix-and-match polyesters for this hot, humid climate was just plain stupid. I envy the smart travelers who move around effortlessly with their backpacks. But I'll struggle with this damn suitcase for just a few more weeks until Bangkok, the end of my road, where I'll buy a cheap ticket to go back home.

It's a scenic, breezy ferry ride to the island of Penang, and I'm delighted that it's free. I catch a trishaw to the Tye Ann hotel, recommended in my guidebook, along with their banana porridge, rated as "Best in South-East Asia."

That sounded like comfort food. And, boy, am I ever hungry for comfort!

The trishaw drops me at the door to the hotel, and I'm told that a room will be opening up later in the afternoon. In another wild coincidence (or maybe synchronicity?), sitting in the restaurant is Pat, the striking, blonde Canadian who so impressed me back at the food court in Singapore.

"Fancy meeting you here!" I say enthusiastically as our eyes meet. I learn that she, too, is waiting for a room to open up, and we immediately agree to be roommates.

It's as if the universe has delivered another angel to guide me. I sheepishly ask Pat if it's okay for me to tag along with her. I know I can learn a lot from this accomplished solo traveler.

"Of course," she readily agrees.

The hotel is a dive, but the porridge is delicious!

This evening, we explore the night market opposite the Queen Victoria Memorial Clock. Hundreds of vendors are selling spices, fruits, fresh seafood, handicrafts, and other goods. I'm deeply immersed in a sea of exotic smells, sounds, and sights. The food stalls fascinate me as I watch busy cooks thread skewers of meat over fiery grills. Octopus tentacles sizzle and colorful veggies are tossed in cast iron woks. And deliciously sweet soy milk is ladled from a steaming kettle.

Sunday, November 19

This morning, Pat and I set off to explore the Temple of the Million Buddhas. I don't count, but that number can't be too far off. The walls of the many-storied pagoda are lined with tiles of Buddha, in addition to a profusion of statues in every direction.

We take public buses all around the beautiful island. We sit and talk at Batu Ferringhi Beach until after sunset. Although she's obviously adventurous, Pat is not as brash and headstrong as some of the other female travelers I've met. She's a bit reserved, down to earth, with a sensible head on her shoulders. In fact, she's a lot like me!

It takes us almost ninety minutes to make bus connections back to George Town. Before returning to the hotel, we stop for something to eat—curry, no less, which I find I'm starting to like.

Pat is a bit of a foodie, and I learn that Malaysian cuisine is a mix of Chinese, Thai, and Indian influences. I share some trivia that I read in my guidebook about a local specialty called "Kurry Kapitan." Supposedly a Dutch sea captain asked his cook what was on that night's menu. The answer: "Curry, Captain." And it's been on menus here ever since!

Monday, November 20

For lunch today, we share grilled meat skewers with *satay* peanut sauce, *laksa* (noodle soup), and a famous salad called *rojak*, which mixes turnips, cucumber, green mangoes, bean sprouts, fried tofu, and green apples with a dressing of sugar, chili, lime juice, and shrimp paste.

Pat giggles as I recount my experience of tasting my first taco—just five years ago—in the Delta College cafeteria. The salsa package was labeled mild, but my mouth was on fire! I had never tasted anything like it before. And here I am, eating turnips and tofu and green mangoes. Me and my taste buds have come a long way!

After lunch, Pat and I spend a few relaxing hours in our hotel room, reading and writing letters. I decide to lighten my load, unpacking my purse and my bags and laying everything out on the bed. I'm motivated to get better organized, once and for all.

Later in the afternoon, when our tummies start to rumble, Pat suggests that we go to a place that serves *murtabak*, which she describes as a kind of pancake stuffed with meat, egg, and vegetables. Hmmmm, pancakes! Though I've never had a pancake that didn't come drenched in maple syrup, I'm willing to try it.

As usual, it's strangely delicious.

Wandering back along Chulia Street, I admire the multicultural-ism of this place. The architecture is British colonial, sprinkled with Indian, Muslim, and Chinese influences. Pat stops to buy some durian fruit from a vendor across from the hotel. I've read about durian—it's big, like a watermelon—covered with spikes. The fruit inside is reputed to be sweet, nutritious, and absolutely delicious—but surprisingly stinky. A smell so putrid, in fact, that the fruit is banned on public transportation in major Asian cities!

I stand in awe as Pat begins her negotiation with the vendor, marveling at how self-assured and adventurous she is. And—at the same time—wondering if she's planning to bring the smelly fruit back to our hotel room.

In the next instant, I feel my purse being grabbed from behind and turn to see a guy running away with it.

I have only one thought: *My passport! He's got my passport!*

Stupidly, when we left the hotel to get some dinner, I had not tucked my passport back into the homemade pouch I keep pinned inside my undies.

Without hesitation, I instinctively sprint after the guy—in my pink flipflops—as he races to the end of the block where his accomplice waits on a motorcycle. I manage to grab onto his shirt collar just as he climbs on board. The driver hits the throttle and starts moving, but I'm still holding tight to the guy's shirt. The driver speeds up—dodging pedestrians and rickshaws on the busy street. I run faster and hang on for dear life, all the while shouting, "Gimme back my purse!"

When my rational mind finally catches up to my instinctive, unthinking action, I have one crazy thought: *Now what do I do?*

The driver rounds a corner, and—to my surprise (and theirs!)—the bike tips over. The driver runs away. My purse skids across the pavement, and I scramble after it, stepping on the strap. As I reach down to grab it, the thief, whom I'll call "Snatcher-Boy," lunges for the bag and knocks me off my feet. I'm now flat on my back on the pavement, clutching my purse firmly against my chest as he struggles to rip it from my grasp.

Amidst this furious scuffle, two surprisingly vivid and unrelated memories pop into my mind: I remember the Lonely Planet guidebook's warning about the prevalence of drug addicts here in Penang, and how one needed to be mindful of thieves. I also recall wrestling matches instigated by my brother, Bob in our living room on Glendale Street when I was growing up.

Moments ago, Chulia Street bustled with shoppers and pedestrians engaged in their evening affairs. But now, the street is devoid of people. It's just me and the thief. I look into his eyes. He's desperate. He's not giving up.

But neither am I.

We struggle some more. Another moment passes before I hear it: A low rumbling that makes the ground shake. In my peripheral vision, I see a hulking figure heading toward us. Whatever it is, it is big. And powerful.

Snatcher-Boy notices it, too. I see his eyes grow wide and he releases his grip on my purse. He stands up and takes a couple of steps, but it's too late.

The hulk is an off-duty cop, as wide as he is tall. He grabs Snatcher-Boy, throws him down against the curb, and starts kicking him.

I gasp. "You can't do that!" I holler as I'm thinking, *It's police brutality!*

Pat suddenly appears, as do dozens of locals who gather around, chattering and pointing at me, like I'm some kind of heroine. A real celebrity.

I'm shaking, but unhurt. Pat ushers me into a nearby restaurant and sits me down. She orders tea and says soothingly, "He should have grabbed *my* bag. I never would have chased him like you did."

A crowd of people are clustered on the street, peering inside and pointing. I cannot believe what just happened—my instantaneous reaction and the fact that I actually caught the thief!

A police car arrives on scene, and they push Snatcher-Boy into the back seat. They direct me to get in the car, too. Pat protests loudly, "No! She's not getting in the same car with him. Tell them to send another car!"

Once again, I'm in awe of her power. But they relent and send another squad car. At police headquarters, I give a detailed verbal statement as well as a written statement. The cops joke about the incident, proudly claiming they watch *Kojak*, a popular American TV series about a bald-headed, tough-but-honest New York police detective.

Snatcher-Boy—a scary-looking character only about twenty years old—is there, too, staring at me. Perhaps he's trying to intimidate me, or perhaps he's amazed that a girl fought back?

The detective asks if I will testify. Apparently, the guy has pled guilty but is still demanding his day in court.

"I was planning to leave to go to Thailand," I say.

"We'll pay you for your time," he says. "And the trial will take place in just a few days."

He had me at, "We'll pay you…!"

"Okay, sure. I guess I can delay my departure a bit."

Later, when Pat and I return to the hotel, I see all my belongings laid out on the bed, just as I'd left them. And there's my passport—sitting prominently on top of the pile!

Tuesday, November 21

I listen as Pat recounts the story to other travelers, blushing each time she retells it. *Was it really me who did that?* I can't deny that I'm feeling victorious. Triumphant. Even a little giddy.

Pat is heading off to Bangkok today. I hug her goodbye and she whispers, "Good luck, Marilyn, and be sure to let me know what happens."

"But we never got to taste the durian fruit!" I say.

"Maybe next time. You never know, we just might cross paths again!"

Wednesday, November 22: Penang High Court

On any other day, I might be visiting this impressive courthouse as a tourist. In 1807, England's King George III granted a Royal Charter for the British East India Company to establish a Court of Justice on this site. Originally a wooden structure with a thatched roof, it was rebuilt in 1903 in the Palladian style featuring a domed central chamber and dozens of classical white columns.

But on this day, I'm no tourist. I'm here to testify at a criminal trial that is happening less than forty-eight hours from the time of the offense. Justice is swift here in Malaysia.

In the traditional wood-paneled courtroom, I suppress a giggle at the sight of Malaysian judges and barristers wearing black robes and powdered white wigs with rows of tight curls—a holdover from the British judicial system.

Snatcher-Boy leers at me from the defense table. He's covered with visible bruises from his police battering. I look back at him with smug self-assurance, thinking, *You never should have messed with me, you jerk!*

I give my testimony from an elevated witness stand as I confidently relay the still-vivid details of the robbery to the judge, who tells me as I conclude my testimony, "I admire you for what you did."

He slams down his gavel. "Guilty!"

The detective and a high-ranking female police officer take me out to lunch and give me an envelope with the promised payment for my time. Four Malaysian ringgit converts to less than two US dollars. But I don't care. I feel triumphant. Powerful. Indomitable. This shy, quiet "good girl" from Saginaw, Michigan, chases down a thief in Malaysia! My new theme song plays in my head: "If My Friends Could See Me Now." I imagine Dad bragging about his little girl to his buddies at Maple Hill Golf Club. And my brother Bob would undoubtedly take credit for training me to fight, claiming that he'd sometimes let me win our living room wrestling matches.

But as much as I'd love to sing my praises, I can't share anything about this experience with anybody back home because they're already plenty worried about me.

The police detective followed through on his promise to let me know about the sentencing. When I returned home months later, there was an envelope containing a newspaper clipping with the headline, "Snatch Thief Gets Three Years." It went on to explain that the thief—an addict— had prior convictions...and he'd be serving his term at hard labor.

Thursday and Friday, November 23–24: To Ko Samui, Thailand

I've never heard of Ko Samui, but Pat—the expert traveler whom I trust implicitly on such matters—told me it was worth the arduous journey to get to this island off Thailand's east coast. It's more than six hours by rail to Hat Yai in southern Thailand, where I connect to a nice third-class train to Surat Thani. I stay in a grungy, but cheap, hotel for the night and then catch the 11 a.m. speedboat out to the island. "Speedboat" is a relative term, I learn. I finally arrive here on Ko (which means "island" in Thai) Samui after 4 p.m.

I'm immediately in love. White beaches, beautiful azure water, coconut palms, clear skies, and—best of all—it's dirt cheap! My bungalow room is only 20 Baht—$1 per night. I'll definitely spend a week here—or maybe forever!

Though I've never been there, I'm thinking Hawaii was probably like this a hundred years ago. The menu at my hotel features fresh fish, vegetables, and delicious tropical fruit, with most entrees under about 75 cents. The breakfast porridge is to die for, too!

Ko Samui is a very free place for the visitor. Girls (not including me) sunbathe and swim in the nude, and pot is sold and smoked openly. A trip into the town to buy some prepaid airgrams at the post office takes me the entire day—such is the pace of life here. I see the Big Buddha (which is really big) and stop to watch a trained monkey scamper up a palm tree, twist free a ripe coconut, and drop it to the ground.

It's so perfect here, but I know it'll change—like everything does.

Even me. I'm noticing that I'm changing, too. Even before I chased down the purse snatcher, I was becoming mindful of my growing independence and confidence. I have a lot of time to think.

I've got to figure out a way to design my life so that I have more opportunities to travel in the future. I've met so many interesting global travelers and learned about many places that I *must* see. Teaching seems like the only option to give me the time off to travel. I'll pursue a teaching job in earnest when I get home.

Which, I've decided, is not necessarily gonna happen by Christmas, as I'd been planning. Sure, that would be delightful for a week—but I'm here in southeast Asia with time and money and many more places to see. I know I'd really regret not seizing this opportunity. So, I'm keeping all options open. Once I get to Bangkok, I'll look into what's next. Given the geography, I have to fly somewhere because I can't proceed further by land route—either north or east into Laos or Cambodia or west into Burma—because such travel is prohibited.

Maybe I'll go to Kathmandu—if only because the lyrics of the Bob Seger song play in my head every time I think about the place! Or maybe India if I can find a travel companion. Maybe Greece after that?

All I know is that I don't have to decide anything today. I'm really getting into this "one day at a time" concept!

Tuesday, November 28

Choeg Choi is an annoyingly persistent—but charming—little teenage hustler who has been my unintended escort and translator since my arrival. He's always at the ready with a suggestion and his pudgy hand held out for a small gratuity. He's got more confidence in his little finger…

At breakfast, he tells me about a movie crew from Bangkok that's here on the island to film scenes of a bullfight.

"You must see," he exclaims excitedly, "and I will arrange for you." He obviously has made the same pitch to travelers staying elsewhere, because an hour later, a small tour bus shows up and fifteen of us pile onboard. First stop is at a beautiful waterfall—where the guys swim in the pool below and us girls just watch, having no swimsuits nor the courage to swim in the nude. Next, we arrive at the filming location, where two male water buffalo, separated only by a curtain, are being erotically "aroused" by their trainers.

I expect the event to last only a few minutes and forcefully position myself in the first row behind the bamboo barrier erected for crowd control. My camera is poised and ready to capture the action when they drop the curtain and the bulls charge at each other, locking horns. But as the crowd surges forward, my foot is painfully pinned under a bamboo pole on which dozens of people are standing, and I cannot get it free. For many minutes, nobody can hear me screaming—nor do they care. All the while I'm panicked to think, *I paid 20 baht to see this bullfight and I'm missing the whole thing!*

Eventually, I dislodge my foot with all five toes still intact. I scurry after the crowd, only to catch sight as the horn of one bull gouges the eyeball of the other.

I need to see no more and turn away, letting the crazy mob get their thrills. As far as I can figure, the entire population of the island is here. I hope the film crew gets the footage they want, since there's not going to be a second take on this set!

On the drive home, we see a gorgeous sunset. And tonight, the stars are shining especially bright. It is *so* beautiful. I am in awe, and I promise myself that I will never forget the grandeur of this fabulous night.

Wednesday, November 29

It's my last full day on this island paradise and I pledge to not waste a moment of it. I get up really early to watch a magnificent sunrise over the Gulf of Thailand. I spend the afternoon writing letters to family and friends back home and socializing with the interesting and adventurous travelers who are here from all over the world.

My "last supper" is memorable and absolutely delicious—the chef's masterpiece: sweet-and-sour fish with vegetables.

The taxi will pick me up at 5 a.m. tomorrow, so I know I should go to bed early, but I must savor every last moment in this magical place. An Aussie traveler shares a couple hits of Thai dope from a homemade bamboo bong. Losing track of time, I leave later than planned. Halfway home, the lights go out precisely on schedule, and I must cross a river to get back to my bungalow in complete darkness. Pretty scary—especially when buzzed!

Friday, December 1: To Bangkok

The overnight train from Surat Thani arrives in Bangkok, on schedule, at 5:10 a.m. Although I hadn't planned it that way, it's a good move because the streets aren't yet too crowded. I've sworn off my stupid suitcase forever…I'm shipping it home and buying a backpack. My ideas about what is absolutely essential have changed substantially in three months.

The Malaysia Hotel is *the* place to stay here. According to my trusty guidebook, it was the favorite of Vietnam servicemen coming to enjoy R&R at a high-rise property with a swimming pool and air-conditioning. But then the war ended, and the hotel had no customers. So, they slash prices to the bone, fill the place with freaks, and do practically no maintenance. The guidebook explains, "It's sort of a working test on how long a building can hang together with much abuse and nobody looking after it."

Apparently, it's more expensive than other Bangkok cheapies, "but most people seem to feel it's worth it." The Malaysia's noticeboard is an Asian travel institution, where one can find out just about anything: black market prices, how to dodge your visa limitations, travelers seeking roommates, fake student IDs, and cures for venereal disease.

I regret not paying extra for a sleeping berth on yesterday's train. I had to get up at 4:30 a.m. to catch the ferry out of Ko Samui, but the overnight train to Bangkok didn't leave Surat Thani till 4:30 in the afternoon. I felt feverish all day and got very little sleep in my terribly uncomfortable third-class seat. But it was only $4. My thrifty side won out again—but at what cost?

I expected to spend the day in bed, but I'm motivated to see the town. Traffic is terrible and the noise is unbearable. I check out several travel agencies, but it's difficult to make plans when one doesn't know where she wants to go! One option is to fly to Calcutta for only $93. But maybe I should start in the south of India, possibly visiting Sri Lanka first. The north of India and Nepal will be very cold right now.

I decide to not decide anything. I've been doing that quite a bit lately.

Not having any firm idea of my timeline, I had told family and friends to send mail to the Peace Corps office here in Bangkok and prayed that they'd hold the mail till I got here to claim it. So, that's my next stop. Yippee—there's a bunch of correspondence! But at the top of the stack is a telegram—from Barbara, who is currently in Penang, advising that she and Harriet will be arriving here in Bangkok on December 5th!

Whoah! After all this time, I never expected that they would ever catch up to me. And I have mixed feelings. I've been enjoying the freedom and independence of solo travel. Making my own decisions without compromising. Not being a third wheel. We'll have to have a heart-to-heart talk about our expectations and see where we all stand. If our ideas and thinking don't correlate, I have no hesitation about traveling alone. And I'm determined that—if we do proceed as a threesome—I will be more assertive and independent than before.

I find a bench in a nearby park to read the correspondence from home. There are three letters from Mom, who hasn't heard from me in a few weeks. She's been in communication with Barbara's mother and now knows that I've been traveling alone—which I'd not shared with her. She also contacted Sheila, who mentioned my concerns about traveling with Harriet. Boy, did *that* ever get blown out of proportion! It's comical to read the progression of correspondence and the distorted, exaggerated ideas that evolved from something I casually mentioned in a letter sent many weeks ago.

I remembered having received a letter from Barbara shortly after she arrived in her Philippine village in 1976. She wrote while in a depressed mood, and I was very concerned about her. So, I understand how things can seem so much worse through the lens with which we view it on the other side of the world.

My friend Jan sent a letter with a bunch of pictures from Sharon's and Patti's weddings. Gosh—I missed weddings that I would have attended—yet again—as a single, unattached girl. Oh, well ….

And Sheila wrote one of her typically succinct letters. She's never short of conversation except when it comes to writing it down!

I'm really glad to be here instead of there. Nothing has changed—not that I expected any different.

Sunday, December 3

I would probably be leaving Bangkok today to head north to Chiang Mai, except that I need to wait for Barbara and Harriet. So, I've got lots of time to think and anticipate our reunion—which is not a good thing. I'm once again feeling insecure and lonely. *Dammit! What happened to my confidence and certainty?*

My feelings are pathetic. I'm needy. Why do my emotions quickly see-saw between weak and strong? I like strong *so* much better. I tell myself that I'm a rookie at this new courageous woman thing. A lifetime of insecurity and looking to others for validation and acceptance isn't just gonna disappear in a matter of weeks.

Tuesday, December 5

It's the King's birthday—a national holiday in Thailand. I'm still lacking energy and an appetite. Barbara and Harriet are supposed to arrive today, but after all the waiting I did back in Singapore, I'm half expecting that they won't show. But I am hopeful—because I'm in dire need of friendship right now.

I get a call in my hotel room from Barbara with the suggestion that we meet later for dinner. She doesn't sound too excited about reconnecting. I'm probably reading too much into our brief conversation. I do that a lot.

Our dinner meeting feels a bit forced. She and Harriet share stories about their experience in Malaysia—disco dancing, partying, and picking up guys. Not my style at all, but they've been socially and geographically isolated for the past two years and the freedom is refreshing.

They share their plan to go to Israel and work on a kibbutz because Barbara's intestinal problems will prevent her from traveling to India.

It's finally becoming clear to me that they're not wrong. Nor am I wrong. I'm "fresh off the boat" and am interested and curious to experience the local lifestyles, while they want only to escape from the "local" lifestyles they've been living for the past two years. With such limited communication options, there was no reasonable way for me to understand what kind of a world I was entering or how Barbara would be different after living for two years in a remote Filipino village.

I'm now crystal clear that my expectations have been unrealistic—and I'm suddenly feeling strong and energized once again to proceed on my own and pursue the activities that I enjoy. It's a powerful awareness!

Wednesday, December 6

It's a productive day today—I'm getting a lot accomplished. I call home to tell my parents of my plan to continue traveling on by myself. My communication is strong and confident, and they don't object or voice any worries—at least not out loud. Later, I do some of the requisite temple touring—the Reclining Buddha and the Emerald Buddha, each elaborate and encrusted with gold and precious stones.

Discovering that no place sells the aluminum-frame backpacks that most low-budget foreign travelers use, I've bought a duffle bag instead. It'll be preferable to my suitcase and shoulder tote, which I ship back home to Michigan, along with nearly everything I had originally brought with me. I enclose a letter to Mom, explaining that this suitcase full of mix-and-match polyesters is not practical for the journey I'm on—a different one than I expected. I tell her I am doing fine and that she shouldn't worry about me. But I know that is futile advice—she will worry, no matter what.

I wanted to share how each day is an adventure with exotic new tastes and interesting new people. And how I'm experiencing a great, big, wonderful world that had eluded me in the comfortable, boring bubble of Midwestern life. And how I'm having more fun and finding more fulfillment than I've ever known. And that there's almost nothing about my former life that I'm missing. But I say none of this in my letter because I don't want to rub it in.

I locate a bookstore and buy the Lonely Planet guidebook, *Across Asia on the Cheap*, which covers Sri Lanka, India, and other parts of Asia that I'll visit next. I go to the Sri Lankan embassy and learn I do not need a visa. I buy a bus ticket for Saturday's twelve-hour overnight transfer to Chiang Mai in the north of Thailand.

I meet up with new friends for steak sandwiches at an English pub restaurant: Finola from Scotland, Mark from Australia, and Albert from California. Afterward, we go to the Sheraton, where we're kicked out because we can't afford their drink prices. Then, we go to a couple of places along Patpong Road, where the sex shows are amazing. I've never imagined that a girl could smoke a cigarette with her vagina! These girls are extremely talented and beautiful, but I'm disturbed about the exploitation.

But the highlight of the evening was when Albert offered to loan me his H-frame backpack! He's heading home to California soon and doesn't need it, so he's happy to pack his stuff in my canvas duffle—and I'll ship the backpack to him when I get back home. What a blessing!

Saturday, December 9: To Chiang Mai

It feels like the beginning of a new adventure! I say goodbye to Barbara and Harriet without a hint of regret, and I'm off!

The overnight bus leaves at 7 p.m., and I take a seat next to a good-looking guy from Edmonton, Canada. Graham has been in Thailand only about two weeks and isn't yet on the local sleep schedule. He's talking and talking while I'm getting sleepier and sleepier…

Sunday, December 10

The bus arrives early this morning, and Graham has told me about a newly opened place called Isra Guest House. Having no definite plan, I agree to share a room (not a bed) with him. Also on our bus is an affable Welshman named Trefor, and we all agree to split the cost of a triple, if they have such accommodations at this place. Such is the priority of the low-budget traveler.

It's a very nice house—quite modern, with a homey feel. We take off our shoes at the door and dump our bags before meeting our housemates: John and Holly, a Canadian couple from Sarnia, Ontario; crazy Peter, a long-haired, pot-smoking, barefoot hippie from California; Dale, a semi-professional golfer from Vancouver who is spending the winter here where it's warmer and cheaper; and Andre and Monique, a French couple.

Bikes are free, so we take off to explore. I'm euphoric! Graham and Trefor are fun company, and Trefor is a hilarious sight with his baggy pants tucked into his socks with a big straw hat on his head!

What a difference a week can make. I'm so happy, it's hard to remember that I was anxious and depressed just days ago.

We buy some fresh fruit in the market to share with our hosts and housemates. The young Thai couple who own our guesthouse, Isra and Mon, are as curious about us as we are about them. And Mr. Noo, their crazy old caretaker, is a hoot. A great start—I'm really gonna like it here!

The next days...

Without a definite agenda or any pressing deadline, I'm free to enjoy these days. I have ample opportunity to use Thai phrases like *"sawatdee ka"* (hello), *"taow rai?"* (how much?), and *"kop kun ka"* (thank you).

One day, I ride about twenty kilometers into the countryside to visit handicraft villages where they make umbrellas and weave cloth. People are busy with the rice harvest, but they smile and wave as I pass. The villages are disappointing—obvious tourist traps—but I'm proud of myself for not buying anything. I've got many more months of travel ahead of me. And what will I do with a fancy umbrella, anyway?

But I'm starting to feel a familiar anxiety—if I'm to be in Sri Lanka for Christmas, I'd better wrap up everything I want to do here and get back to Bangkok to book a flight. One night, over bottles of Singha beer with Graham and Trefor, I share my trepidation about leaving a place I've grown to love. I'm relieved to learn they both feel the same way. It's so pleasant here, and so much fun—but it's not gonna last forever. Eventually, we'll all split up and go our separate ways.

I have a chat with Isra about booking a trek up into the hill tribe region north of here. John and Holly are also interested, but they want to do a longer trek—staying a few days in each of the villages instead of the standard routing, which includes one-night stays with each of a few tribes.

Their plan appeals to me, too. So, I make the decision to *not* leave Thailand before Christmas—especially since there's no way to know if there will be any available seats on a flight. I'll stay here at Isra House for the holidays—celebrating with these people I've grown fond of. We can plan a fun Christmas party—sharing some of our own traditions with our Buddhist hosts.

Isra reassures us that it will be okay to begin trekking with an organized group and just remain in the first village for an extra night or two until the next group comes through.

Saturday, December 16: To the Hill Tribes

This morning we meet our tour guide, Dang, and four other trekkers. The first leg of our itinerary is easy—we are driven for an hour to a village of the Karen tribe. It's a dusty village with shy, inquisitive people. On her porch, an old lady is weaving on a back-strap loom. Nearby, I watch in amazement as a tiny woman drops a heavy wooden pestle onto a stone mortar bowl containing raw rice. Over and over, she repeats this procedure to separate the husk from the kernel.

This is what is required to prepare rice? Once again, I experience one of those moments of awe and wonderment. Had I been borne to different parents, I might be living a lifestyle similar to this, weaving my own cloth and pounding raw rice instead of dashing to the fabric store or supermarket for what I need.

Dang explains that the Karen tribespeople are originally from China, having migrated to Laos and, later, here to Thailand. This village is approximately twenty years old, with a population of about two hundred. Houses are made of bamboo, wood, and thatch and raised on stilts. Married women wear dark sarongs in predominantly red colors with a special dark jacket. Unmarried women—mostly girls—wear white dresses trimmed in red. Women are the head of the family and men are the head of the village. When I ask why there are no men around, Dang explains, "They're probably out in the woods collecting roots and bark to sell in town for medicine and natural dyes."

On the road again, traveling to the next village, we pass an elephant! We cannot resist acting the part of typical tourists, piling out of the jeep to take photos.

Next, we arrive at the trailhead for a one-hour trek—uphill all the way. Huffing and puffing, we finally reach a village of the Black Lahu. I expect them to be shy like the tribe of Karens we'd just visited. But no—we're immediately surrounded by little kids, babbling and climbing on our backs asking for cigarettes. Their aggression is a bit overwhelming, and it's disturbing to see the kids smoking. But the novelty of our being here wears off after a while.

We'll be sleeping at the house of the brother of the tribal chief. We're served tea and noodle soup for lunch. Dang explains that the Black Lahu emigrated from Tibet to Burma to Thailand about eighty years ago, and this particular village has been here for twenty years. Their religious belief is animism—they fear ghosts and spirits. The village chief is the political leader, the animist chief is the spiritual leader, and the customs chief is in charge of maintaining tradition.

Young kids are given a baby pig to raise. When the pig is old enough to slaughter, the child is old enough to marry—and the pig is eaten at the marriage celebration. Marital age is between fifteen and twenty, and boys choose the girl they want to marry—but girls can refuse. Divorce is acceptable but not common.

The Black Lahu tribe grows opium poppies, but the government is encouraging them to grow coffee instead. However, transporting coffee beans to market is a challenge because there are no roads. Dang explains that about a third of the population smokes opium, with some old men smoking two-to-three hundred pipefuls every day! Again, the Thai government is discouraging this lifestyle for the younger generation—hence the consumption of cigarettes.

After dinner, Nasue, the wife, makes each of us a woven grass bracelet for which we pay her two baht. Jasong, her husband, demonstrates opium smoking to those of us curious to try a pipeful.

Sunday, December 17

The next afternoon, we hike uphill to see a poppy field. Now, I know why they call them hill tribes! A few poppies are blossoming with purple and white flowers. Other crops are mixed in coffee, castor oil, ginger root, and soybeans.

Some women and girls share sugarcane with us. Their large packs, filled with vegetables and firewood, have a strap which stretches across their forehead as they lumber up and down the hills with their heavy burden.

The bathroom is in the woods, and they bathe in the ice-cold creek. I can see why these people prefer to just stay dirty!

Clothes are predominantly black with tiny, intricate strips of colorful cloth sewn as trim on sleeves and hem, across shoulders, and up the side seams. Nasue demonstrates some of the handiwork on a piece of cloth—in very exacting, tedious detail. *Wouldn't mind trying to do some of it myself,* I think.

Babies wear cute, colorful caps and kids are as agile as mountain goats. Dogs are a real menace here as they bark at us constantly, snarling and showing their teeth.

We go down to the creek to wash, and the kids all want to brush their teeth. They've obviously done it before because they ask us for toothpaste. It's dark by 6 p.m. and extremely chilly. I'm grateful to have rented a down sleeping bag—otherwise, I'd make this a two-night trek.

Dang has taken a liking to me and has made several references regarding "sleeping close together to keep warm." He does get a bit amorous after the lights go out, but, thankfully, a simple "no" is enough.

Monday, December 18

I arise on this chilly morning to eat breakfast of cold fried eggs and toast. This is when Dang and the other trekkers in our group will move on, leaving John, Holly, and me behind in this village. Dang seems very anxious not to leave us (or perhaps me) here. He gives us some bread and coffee, with instructions to not smoke any more opium!

The family agrees to feed us rice and vegetables at lunch and dinner, so we will not starve. It's hard to believe that this is real life and not a simulation for the tourists. No one in the village speaks English, so we're on our own. We have only a few words and phrases translated into Thai for us to communicate with the villagers.

But two other trekking groups come through the village today, spoiling my idealized notion of being isolated from civilization. Supposedly, this village was added to itineraries only a month ago.

The Black Lahu people are curious, especially about our possessions. They are intrigued by John and Holly's shiny aluminum cook set. They think the knives are like razors for cutting hair.

I am impressed with family life here. Jasong, does much of the cooking and he also takes care of the kids. Today he's gone off to the woods to slash and burn—a system of cutting trees and burning brush that creates tillable open space for farming, but, as a consequence, devastates the land.

Nasue, being a very enterprising lady, puts her three guests to work. We spend well over an hour in the midday sun shucking beans—separating the red beans from the dried husk. I feel useful and productive for the first time on this trip! So many times during these past few months in Asia, I've felt a deferential attitude from the locals—as if foreign visitors are so much "better" than them. But these tribal people believe themselves to be superior to everyone, which is unusual and refreshing.

Later in the afternoon, we are again called out to help. This time the whole family is involved: Nasue and Jasong's children as well as some neighbor kids, along with the three of us, are laboring on a bamboo platform, working together to shuck castor oil beans before sunset. I find it interesting that the kids need no prodding to get them to work. Rarely do I hear scolding, crying, or tantrums.

Jasong is very interested in learning some English. After dinner, before bedtime, we all sit around the kitchen fire communicating in sign language, elementary Thai, and broken English.

I have a chance to play one of their instruments—a huge thing made of bamboo poles attached to a giant gourd. Blowing through the neck of the gourd, I use my fingers to cover holes bored into the bamboo. I've never been musically inclined, so everyone is relieved when I finally give up!

There's a small school with two classrooms, one of which has a map of Thailand, a Thai alphabet chart, and a drawing of a chili plant on the chalkboard. And, of course, the requisite portrait of King Rama IX. Kids attend school infrequently, whenever they're not doing chores or taking care of younger children.

As agreed, they feed us rice and vegetables for lunch and dinner. Now I recognize how monotonous is their diet, given the limited variety they have on hand. But we have some tuna and cheese to liven up our meals and add some protein.

After dinner, Nasue has read my mind: she hands me her needlework when her baby starts to fuss. She points at the small rows of running stitches and indicates I'm to copy her work. The lighting is poor and it's difficult to see what I'm doing. But my handiwork is obviously acceptable because she refuses to take it back when I offer!

Tuesday, December 19

I spend another mostly sleepless night due to the cold. We're expecting Dang to arrive here today and will depart with his group tomorrow morning to trek up to the Akha village. But Dang shows up early this afternoon to collect us, explaining that tonight is a big celebration in another village—one not to be missed. We scurry to get our things together and say goodbye and thanks to Nasue and Jasong. Later, Dang tells us that they said guests like us were welcome to spend a month with them. It's good to know we were so well-liked.

After about two-and-a-half hours, hiking mostly uphill, we arrive at the Akha village, which looks more primitive than the Black Lahu. Some women and girls are attired in elaborate costumes and head-dresses, but most boys and men wear western garb.

Dang explains that tonight's celebration will take place at the "embracing ground," where pubescent girls and boys practice free love. The "love gate" contains all kinds of phallic symbols and erotic carvings we are forbidden to touch.

I'm both fascinated and frustrated with the ceremony. Fascinated with the open sexuality among these very young kids. But frustrated that the boys are all drinking rice whiskey to celebrate the new year and are blatantly checking out the girls from top to bottom. And I wonder if this "meat market" mentality is tradition—or learned from western society?

After marriage, we're told that the husband sleeps in one room and the wife stays in another part of the house behind a partition. They do have large families, but when they get it together, I don't know.

The house where we are staying is very gloomy. It has no windows because the Akha are afraid of ghosts. The floor is made of bamboo slats which are not fastened down, so they continually shift around.

Compared to the Black Lahu culture, gender roles are very lopsided in favor of the male. Women do most of the work. The man we're staying with started smoking opium early in the morning, takes a short break in the afternoon, and then resumes his horizontal position each evening. With a glazed look in his eyes, he fills his pipes illuminated by the light of a small kerosene lamp.

Wednesday, December 20

After a restless night trying to sleep on a floor made of bamboo slats, I am awakened by what sounds like a squealing pig. Turns out it *is* a squealing pig. I peek outside my hut just in time to see two guys restraining a large pig, as a third guy wields a large knife. Horrified, I duck back inside…and the pig squeals no more.

I don't witness the actual killing, but I watch them sear off the hide over a blazing fire and then butcher the pig, using every part—tail, intestines, blood, snout, and so on. It's quite a ritual—everything is carefully weighed out to ensure that each of the village's fifteen families will receive an equal portion.

They insist upon sharing some of their feast with us, so I have an unexpected opportunity (for the first and only time in my life!) to taste raw pork with chilies and fried blood—for breakfast!

The Akha bathe only once a year because they're afraid of water spirits. This is that time of year—although if any of them had washed, it isn't obvious. Unfortunately, this village has been spoiled by tourism. Kids blatantly ask for money and cigarettes, and old women try to sell anything and everything. Nobody seems to be working. Perhaps it's because of the holiday, but they strike me as unproductive, with none of the pride of the Black Lahu tribe we just visited.

It's interesting how different these tribes are from one another. Given that they have little opportunity for interaction or connection, tribal cultures and traditions have not been corrupted—except, of course, by the presence of western tourists. I'm infuriated by one German guy with a fancy movie camera who inserts himself into some of the traditional dances, directing the movements and the flow. Another guy is distributing passport pictures of himself to the little kids.

I'm conflicted. Our presence is probably beneficial in some ways, assuming that the tour companies provide fair compensation to the villagers for their hospitality. But our impact is undeniable—and is especially evident in this Akha village where little kids have become annoying beggars.

An old woman comes by selling some dope, so Dang picks out a handful and offers her five baht. We thought it was pretty poor stuff at first. It didn't smell too strong and there wasn't much left after cleaning it. But three good size joints made the rounds of seven of us, and did we *ever* get wasted!

I've never been this high before. An Australian guy starts to hallucinate and his girlfriend giggles hysterically. Dang starts to lose it, and I am using all my concentration just to maintain. John and Holly go to the Love Garden to see the dancing, but I know I can't handle walking down there. I'm trying really hard to bring myself down by drinking cup after cup of tea and coffee. At one point, I fall partway through a hole in the bamboo flooring, which we all find hysterically funny.

Eventually, I manage to get outside and walk around, which is much more difficult than it sounds. I wish I could do it over and enjoy it more.

Thursday, December 21

Another breakfast of too much toast, as we wait for Dang to have his Thai breakfast across the street—which includes rice whiskey. Then, we set off: grateful to be going downhill for a change.

It isn't until we reach the bottom that we learn that the group of trekkers about ten minutes ahead of us has been robbed by armed bandits who stole their watches, cameras, and lots of money. They hit everyone in the group, including the tour guide, Wat.

Somehow, Dang found out about the robbery soon after it happened, but he doesn't say anything to us. Instead, he keeps badgering us to "Keep going. Don't stop." I'm surprised that we didn't get robbed also.

After spending five hours at the local police station, we get back to Isra House—filthy dirty in the same jeans I've been wearing day and night for six days. Feels good to be home after a memorable and worthwhile experience.

Late December: Chiang Mai, Thailand

Christmas holidays have always been my favorite time of year, and even though I'm delighted with my current nomadic lifestyle, I'm anticipating a bit of homesickness. We chat about holiday time one night at dinner, and I'm thrilled that Graham, Peter, Dale, and the French couple will stay here with Isra and Mon to spend Christmas as a "family." Mon has never celebrated Christmas and is very excited to learn about our western traditions—almost like a kid.

Turns out that Graham is quite the cook, so he's planning our Christmas menu. Without a thought, I volunteer to make pumpkin pie.

I don't admit that I've never made a pumpkin pie in my life. But I'm a Home Ec major—I can do this!

The reality of my spontaneous volunteering soon kicks in. For starters, I don't have a recipe. But there's a bookstore in the business district of Chiang Mai where I locate a Betty Crocker cookbook and I copy the recipe. Progress!

It calls for canned pumpkin puree, which is not available here, but they sell fresh pumpkins in the market. I buy whole spices—cinnamon sticks, cloves, and nutmeg—at an Indian medicinal shop and grind them into powder with a wooden mortar and pestle. A square cake pan will substitute for a round pie plate. The other ingredients—flour, eggs, cream, and butter—are easily sourced.

Now…all I need is an oven!

Thai kitchens don't have ovens. Most everything is cooked in a wok or on a barbecue. But a traditional western-style oven? No.

Fortunately, Dale regularly plays golf with some wealthy ex-pats who live in a new western-style housing complex just outside of town. He asks one of his buddies if they have an oven—and the guy says yes.

I show up at their doorstep the day before Christmas—my bicycle basket laden with a pumpkin and all the other ingredients. The lady of the house seems rather put out. Apparently, there was an assumption that I would show up with a pre-made pie to simply pop in their oven for an hour. Nobody has mentioned that I am literally starting from scratch.

The pressure is on!

While the raw pumpkin bakes, I measure the spices with a wild guesstimate as to what constitutes "pumpkin pie spice." Then, it's on to the pastry. I envision the beautiful sheet of dough that Mom would carefully lay down in her pie plate. By comparison, my dough is a sticky, buttery mess that I press crudely into the corners of the cake pan and put in the refrigerator to chill.

It doesn't help that my hostess periodically pops into the kitchen to assess my progress. She's got her own dinner to prepare, and I'm screwing up her timeline.

A few hours later, I tidy up the kitchen and extend profuse apologies and thank-yous to my hosts for their generosity. Balancing my pumpkin creation in the bicycle basket, I carefully pedal back to the guesthouse.

Mon has decorated a tropical bush with colorful candies and letters cut from crepe paper to spell out *"Merry Christmas."* She is beyond excited!

I help Peter cut up fresh papaya, mango, banana, and pineapple for the fruit salad. I watch Isra make Sukiyaki: into each bowl he layers green veggies, beef, and squid which has been gently boiling in a broth. To this, he adds cooked rice and vermicelli noodles, filling bowls to the top with the piping hot broth. He adds a weak mix of Thai chili to the bowls of us foreigners, and a more potent version (with six times more chilies!) for the locals.

Mr. Noo, flaunting a colorful halter top and skirt, tends to the chicken on the barbecue. The French couple makes crepes, which we slather with lemon juice and sugar. There are bowls of peanuts and sweets, as well as copious amounts of Mekhong whiskey, of which Mr. Noo has more than his fair share. Everyone is in a festive mood, further enhanced by marijuana Thai sticks, of which Peter has more than *his* fair share. Someone offers Indonesian clove cigarettes, about which Peter hilariously comments: "It's better than smoking a ham!"

Happily, my pumpkin pie is absolutely terrific! And I'm not the least bit homesick!

Sunday, January 7, 1979: Back to Bangkok

I'm on my way back to Bangkok on a luxury bus, having decided not to travel on the cheap for a change. I've enjoyed five wondrous weeks in Chiang Mai at Isra House. This place has been like home— only better than the home where I grew up. Saying goodbye was not without tears and a promise that, "I will return!" But I know it would never be the same. Never as meaningful as these weeks have been. Never as life-defining as this experience has been.

This trip is sure different from what I expected. Traveling solo was inconceivable. I had never even gone to a movie by myself. But here I am, on a bus in the middle of Thailand—all by myself—with plans to continue my journey to India…*India!* All by myself!

When I started this trip, I was hoping that some of Barbara's confidence and self-assurance would rub off on me. People always labeled me as a sweet, innocent thing—a label that I hated because it marked me as boring and uninteresting. And maybe I was.

But I don't feel that way anymore. I've had a chance to really be *me* with people who have no preconceived impressions about me. I've made friends with men and women who like me for *me.* I can't think of the last time I groped for something to say, afraid of coming across as inadequate or inferior.

There's a good-looking Thai guy across the aisle, and I allow myself to fantasize a bit. It's been a long time since I've thought about or yearned for any kind of romantic encounter. My relationships on this journey have been platonic and friendly, even though there have been plenty of opportunities for hanky-panky if that was my thing.

I've come to the realization that I'm not a Cosmo girl, not a vamp, not sexy or alluring or mysterious. I'm a good girl—a *nice* girl—and it's okay! I'm starting to appreciate that I'm down-to-earth, attractive (but a little heavy), and gutsy. I'm intelligent and considerate. All things that are more important and (hopefully) more attractive to any man I might get involved with in the future.

My hope is that I'll continue this new wave of confidence and self-satisfaction when I return home and not fall into the same old ruts and patterns as before. It'll probably be a challenge because my friends and family will naturally expect the old Marilyn. People won't be aware of any changes in me unless I show them!

But I don't have to worry about that yet—because I'm not going home. I'm going on—to Sri Lanka and then India. New adventures await!

Wednesday, January 17: Arrive Colombo, Sri Lanka

First impressions of Sri Lanka (which changed its name from Ceylon only seven years ago): It's extremely hot and humid. The locals are very dark skinned compared to the Thais. I see workers in bare feet and ox-drawn carts on the streets. There's a strong Portuguese influence in the architecture. Streets are teeming with pedestrians. Women wear colorful saris and men wear sarongs. There are cute little vintage black taxis everywhere—mostly of the British brand, Morris Minor. According to my guidebook, imports of new, non-agricultural vehicles have been banned by the Sri Lankan government since the early 1960s. This means they have to keep vintage cars—like these little black taxis—running for a long time. It looks like a movie scene.

A friendly girl from California is on my flight, so Nancy and I share a taxi to Hotel Nippon, a charming old place. Nancy has friends here

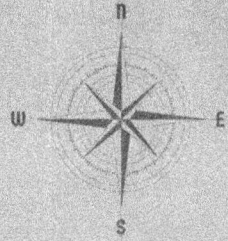

who gather together before dinner. Immediately, I feel out of place…
like a tag-along. Well, I suppose I *am* a tag-along. Nancy's friends are
of the laid back, free-thinking California crowd with faddish ideas to
which I cannot relate. I feel so square around these freaky people, with
their head scarves, vests, eyeliner, and loads of jewelry.

I can handle it for the time being, but I'm anxious to get out on
my own.

Thursday, January 18: Hikkaduwa

Nancy has invited me to join her and a few of her friends on the drive
down to the coastal resort of Hikkaduwa. The driver of our hired car is
Rohan, a very intelligent guy who worked on ships and has seen a lot
of the world. At a rest stop, he and I have a chance to chat privately,
and I tell him that I'm not part of that crowd.

"I'm glad about that," he says. "I didn't think you fit in. Are you
staying with them?"

"No, I'm not. I've got a few places marked in my guidebook, but
I will figure it out when I get there," I respond.

"Let me help you," he says. "I can recommend a couple of decent
places that are not expensive."

I settle on the aptly named Homely Guesthouse, which is only
fifteen rupees per night. It's nothing special, but I'm glad to have
somewhere to hang my hat.

Rohan tells me he'll look me up next time he's here and offers to
let me stay for free at his mother's house when I return to Colombo.

Once again, I'm lucky to have found the right person at the right
time to help me out.

Hikkaduwa is a beautiful place, but I don't like it here. Too much
skin showing on the beach—lots of topless woman and a few totally

naked bodies, and I'm self-conscious about my fat legs. However, I do think my boobs are better than most I'm seeing!

Everyone seems to know everyone else. Lots of French and German couples here, many with their kids. But I haven't met anyone I'm too anxious to get to know.

Lillian, my landlady, brings me tea in the evening and keeps me company. She admires all of my possessions and hints that she'd love me to leave some of them behind. She's fascinated with my wallet with all its compartments and closures, my razor, my deodorant, and my plastic scrub brush. Once again, I become aware of how little most people in the world have—at least in the way of "stuff."

Friday, January 19

It's proof of my stubborn side, that part of me that refuses to give up. Up till now, I'd been intimidated by the food—the fiery hot curries I'd read about. The guidebook described Sri Lankan curries as, "very (very) hot." But on this night, seated in a tiny restaurant filled with locals, I decide to prove that I'm not your average tourist—I am a *traveler!* So, I ask my waiter to bring me what everyone else is eating. He raises his eyebrows but soon returns, placing a section of fresh green banana leaf on the table in front of me, onto which he puts a blob of steaming rice and heaping spoonfuls of four different curries.

After he returns to the kitchen, I notice that I've become the restaurant's big attraction. All eyes are on me. They are encouraging eyes. I am hungry and I dig into my dinner, scooping with my right hand (as the left hand is considered unclean). Within seconds, I feel as though a swarm of fire ants is stinging my mouth. My nose begins to run and my eyes start tearing up. It is miserable, but I'm feeling as if I have the honor of the West to defend. Damned if I am going to let this fiery curry get the better of me! So, I work my way through this banana leaf platter from hell, and when I finish the last mouthful, I feel as if everyone should be on their feet drowning me in cheers.

They don't.

So, I just get up and pay for the meal with a bow and a smile. I can't wait to get back to my room to blow my nose!

Sunday, January 21

I was propositioned on the beach this morning by a seventeen-year-old boy, who asked, "Lady, you want to try one time a Singhalese boy?"

No thanks!

I wonder how many times he's made such an offer—and how many times it's been accepted.

Monday, January 29

I call home today, but I only have three minutes since I can't call collect. I catch Mom at a bad time, and she scares me with an emotional plea to, "Get on a plane and come home." I press her for specifics. There's nothing wrong—she just misses me.

She really hit the old guilt nerve. And it doesn't get better when I mention that I probably won't be home till about Easter time.

She does manage to share some news: my sister-in-law had a baby boy, Danny, on the same day that Aunt Bernice died of a heart attack. And Barbara is coming home this weekend, having run out of money in Europe.

Boy, that is *not* what she wanted, since a big priority was delaying her return to Michigan until after winter.

The three-minute call ends abruptly, and I'm left feeling angry. *Dammit!* I wish she would understand how important this trip is to me. Will I *ever* be free to make my own decisions without family interference?

I spend the rest of the afternoon in a frenzy. I fire off a letter to Sheila, expressing my frustration. And then, I write a carefully worded, eloquent appeal to Mom. I try to explain how my journey is far from a frivolous flit around the world but rather a precious learning experience. And how grateful I am to have this opportunity when most of the people I meet will rarely venture farther than the next village. And how my limited budget forces me to travel on local; i.e., slow modes of transport. Not sure my letter will do any good, but I feel better.

Tuesday, January 30: To Haldummulla

I wake up early to catch the bus to a place in the central highlands that has beautiful sunrises, but, after reaching the depot, I learn that the bus doesn't leave till 11 a.m. As usual, a crowd gathers around me, and I get lots of offers to help. As it turns out, I'm glad to have gotten here so early because I get a seat on the crowded bus, which will take *six* hours to reach Haldummulla! For some reason, I thought it would be only three hours. But it's worth it, as we pass through gorgeous tea estates. I get a big dorm room all to myself—with a spectacular vista out front of lush hills, beautiful gardens, and breathtaking tea plantations.

The next few days are lazy ones. There's a British guy, Owen, staying next door who has been good company. We buy a big jackfruit at the market, combining it with several other yummy tropical fruits to make a delicious salad. I am cognizant that I'm probably doing this to avoid eating curry, which has traumatized me just a bit!

Owen has a good pair of binoculars, which are great for studying the beautiful surroundings of this place.

Saturday, February 3

I find some motivation today to make the trip to World's End—a seven-thousand-foot-high viewpoint with a spectacular drop-off into the valley. In addition to a crazy, hair-raising bus ride, I take a two-and-a-half-hour trek through dense forest and open grasslands where the complete silence is broken only by the buzzing of insects, occasional monkey noises, and the wind. It's a really good day!

Monday, February 5

I've moved on to Nuwara Eliya, in the center of the tea-growing highlands. It's reputed to be a little like England, as it was favored by the British and Scottish pioneers of the tea industry. I've never been to England, so I don't know if that's accurate, but there are a number of bungalows that look like they don't belong here. I'm staying at the Molesworth for 7½ rupees per night—only about 50 cents! Certainly, cheaper than England would be!

I visit one of the tea estates to watch the pickers, mostly women attired in brightly colored saris. I wish I had some film, as the scene would make a striking photograph. But, as with so many other experiences on this trip, I must etch the photo into my memory. I'm disappointed that nothing is happening inside the tea factory, and I learn that they work only during the night. But I see the machines where the workers roll, sift, dry, and grade the various tea leaves. The place smells fantastic.

I've never been a tea drinker, but I just might start after today!

Later, I take the train to Kandy, but nobody has told me that I need to switch trains. Fortunately, I've only gone past the connection point by a couple of stops. Oh, the joys of low-budget travel!

One of the attractions in Kandy is the Temple of the Tooth. According to my guidebook, one of Buddha's pearly whites is reputed to be housed in the temple, but the Portuguese claim to "have destroyed the tooth in the process of making the country fit for Christians."

That bit of trivia reminds me of all the times I sat in class at St. Stephens as Sister Something-Or-Other would exalt the Catholic missionaries who risked their lives spreading the gospel to the heathens of the world. Not knowing any better, I was proud to put my coins in the mission donation envelopes, believing that the missionaries were doing good. But now that I've experienced how imperialism and Christianity have negatively impacted these Asian cultures, I'm more than a little incensed by the concept.

Exploring the market, I bump into Owen, and we repeat our delicious tradition by purchasing mountains of fresh fruit and a big clay pot of homemade curd. The fruit salad is unforgettable!

He and I make a plan to go to Colombo in a few days because my visa is expiring.

Thursday, February 8: Colombo

Owen and I both fall asleep on the evening train and the conductor has to wake us up when we arrive at the capital city of Colombo! Our taxi driver with hairy ears takes us from place to place until we find an acceptable room.

And then, Owen spoils everything by inviting me to share his bed. *Damn him!*

Friday, February 9

I wish I were on my own again. Owen is really starting to annoy me. He's walking too fast and talking too softly, and I'm glad this is the end of the road for us. He's probably pissed at me for not accepting his "invitation" last night, and I'm pissed at him for making it.

The visa runaround is—as expected—a frustrating, complicated bureaucratic process, but now it's done, and I can stay here in Sri Lanka legally for another month.

I'm on the evening train back to Kandy, once again accompanied by an unwanted Singhalese "helper." I don't like being rude, but sometimes, it's the only way to get rid of guys like him. A couple of weeks ago, I'd been pleased to meet a very nice guy who accompanied me to the night bazaar in Hikkaduwa—until I found out he had a seventeen-year-old wife and a baby at home! He was all apologetic, explaining that he wanted to take me home to meet her, but I wanted no part of it.

After that, I'm learning to be less trusting of anyone offering to help me. But I don't like being so cynical.

Sunday, February 11: Kandy

The Botanical Gardens here are beautiful, with huge bamboo groves, giant coconut palms, spectacular yellow bougainvillea trees, colorful orchids, and hundreds of screeching bats through it all. Mom would love it here. (Well, she probably wouldn't love the screeching bats...)

In anticipation for my arrival in India, I'm reading *Freedom At Midnight*. I'm in tears as I finish reading about the events surrounding Indian independence, beginning with the appointment of Lord Mountbatten as the last Viceroy of British India in 1947 and ending with the assassination and funeral of Mahatma Gandhi.

Wednesday, February 14

Today, I'm off to the ancient fortress at Sigiriya, built atop a massive rock outcropping in the fifth century by a prince who buried his father alive in order to seize the throne. He hid here from his brother, rightful heir to the throne, who wanted to extract vengeance. *Geez, what a story!* Walls are decorated with colorful frescoes, mostly of nymph-like women who were part of the king's harem. It's an engineering marvel, with water piped from the base of the mountain 600 feet up to the castle at the top. The guide explained about the extensive network of gardens, reservoirs, and other structures that have given this place UNESCO World Heritage status.

Yet another spectacular place we Americans have never heard of.

Saturday, February 17: Arrive India!

Mysterious, elusive, intense, intimidating India—here I come!

There's a little finger of land extending from northwestern Sri Lanka that probably once touched the little finger of land that extends from southeastern India. I'm glad to have spent last night in the port town of Talaimannar. I'm feeling rested and ready for whatever is to come.

The ferry trip over isn't as decrepit as I feared, probably because "whities" like me are required to purchase first-class tickets. The crossing takes only a few hours, but the Customs and Immigration formalities on either end make it a ten-hour event, from about 7 a.m. to 5 p.m. The pier in the Indian town of Rameswaram is not deep enough for our ferry to dock, so we must transfer to a smaller wooden fishing boat. I feel like I'm arriving in India like some kind of refugee.

I'm definitely in a new place. Unpaved roads, horse-and-buggy taxis, sacred cows, Hindu temples, and processions with their elaborate gods. And lots of people who pay no attention to this bewildered white girl.

Looking for a place to stay, I learn that it's the holy festival of Maha Shivratri and pilgrims have flocked here from all over India

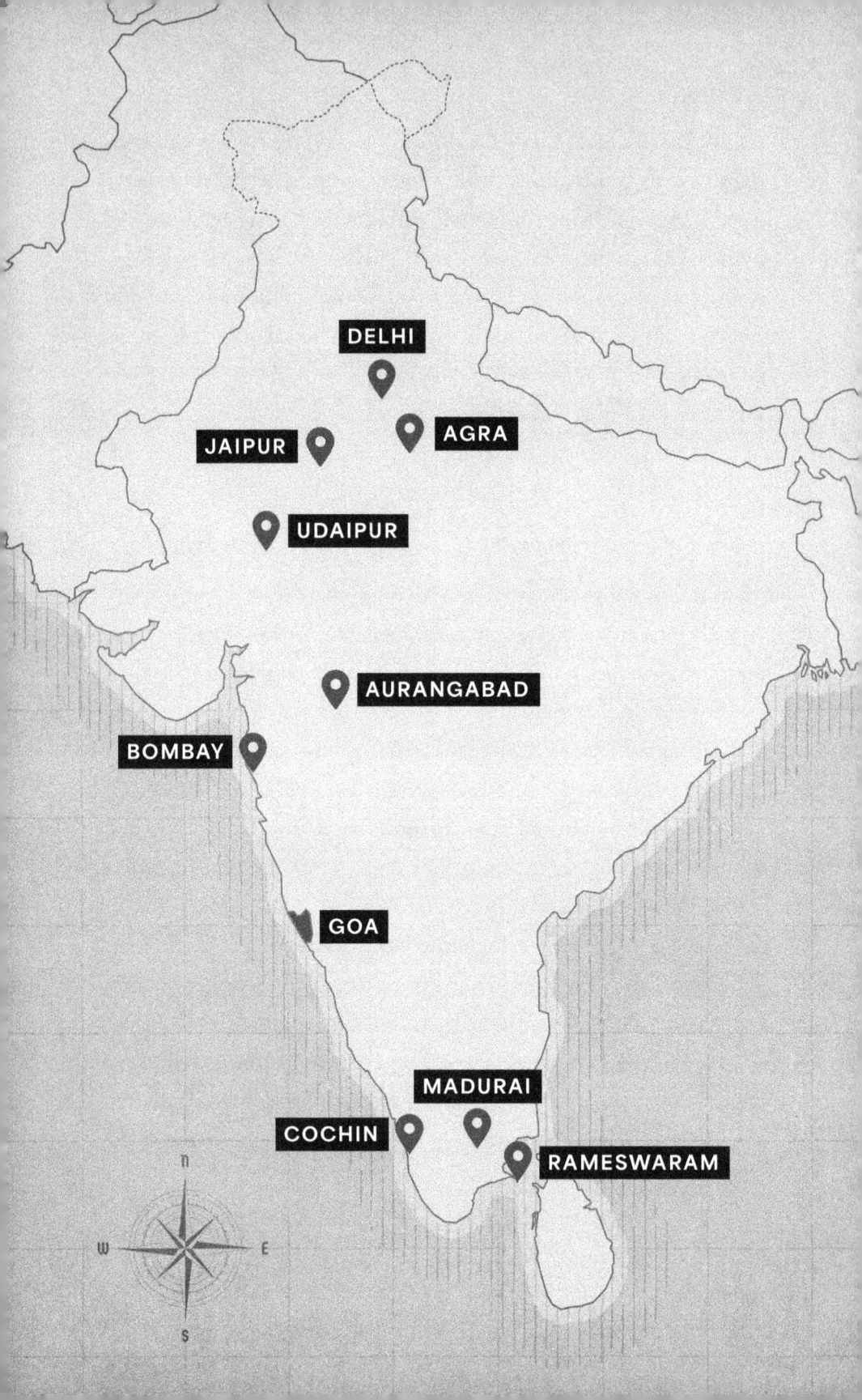

DELHI

JAIPUR AGRA

UDAIPUR

AURANGABAD

BOMBAY

GOA

MADURAI

COCHIN RAMESWARAM

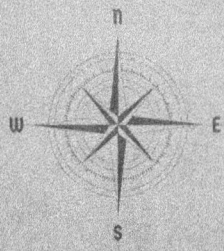

to honor the union of Goddess Parvati with Lord Shiva. Hotels and guesthouses are fully booked—except one place, where I'm shown a room with a concrete floor and rattan mat. And for this, I'm supposed to pay money?

But I'm out of options, so I take the room for my first night—figuring I might need to get used to such crude accommodations in this country. And I'm nervous about the food, so my dinner is a banana and a biscuit. Maybe my diet starts today?

I'll reserve my opinions about India, as I'm sure this grubby little port city isn't typical (at least I hope not!).

Sunday, February 18: Traveling to Madurai

I get up at 5 a.m. to catch the 5:40 train to Madurai, the closest big city on the map, but the guy at the ticket window says the train doesn't go to Madurai. I'll have to wait until 3:45 p.m. *Shit!*

I spend a few minutes in angry frustration before getting back in the ticketing queue. Upon reaching the front, I tell the guy to sell me a ticket on the next train out of here—no matter where it goes!

So, ticket in hand, I board the train and am pleased to find a seat. But I have no idea where I'm going until a fellow passenger explains I can take a bus to Madurai from a place he names with about eight syllables.

We pass through scrubby countryside with plenty of impoverished-looking people. I've been traveling for more than five months through third-world countries, but India has a particular reputation as being the poorest. I don't know if it's true, and I have no way to accurately compare. Not that it matters. Everywhere I've traveled, I've been surprised to discover some of the happiest, most contented people I've ever met. They don't have a lot of stuff but also don't have the stress and competition that we live with in America.

My first experience with Indian public transport is a good one. My train never gets crowded, and when I find my bus at the city with eight syllables, they sell only as many tickets as there are seats—no more.

Arriving in Madurai, I get a nice room at the Ruby Lodge for only 7 rupees (85 cents).

After a much-needed nap, I go to the Meenakshi Temple which is a major pilgrimage site for the Hindus. The guide shows us the Hall of a Thousand Pillars (with 997 pillars!) and umpteen sculptures of their gods and goddesses. I'm sure I'll see lots more holy sites over the course of my stay—but I'm hungry.

So far, I've eaten only bananas and biscuits since arriving in India. Tonight, I have my first chapati with a curry sauce and a delicious yogurt drink called lassi. It's so tasty that I order a second one.

Walking around, I get a good feeling about this place. Street vendors are selling all kinds of things. There are not too many beggars or cars—but look out for the trishaws! The central part of town looks pretty modern. But probably the best part is that I'm anonymous. I expected to be hassled and harried everywhere I went. But that hasn't happened. At least so far.

One thing they do here in India: they tilt their head from side to side, which in our culture means "I don't know," but here it means "yes." That's gonna take some getting used to.

Wednesday, February 21

The bus to Kattayam is scheduled to leave at 9 a.m., but it doesn't show up till 11:15. It's a nice ride through the beautiful Cardamom Hills region, lush with plantations growing coffee, pepper, and cardamom.

We pass the sign for the Periyar Wildlife Reserve in a downpour, and I'm glad not to be getting off at this stop. I make a mental note to see its tigers and elephants next time I come to India!

Arrive at Kottayam at 7:15 p.m.—just in time to catch the bus to Cochin, which is supposed to depart at 7:35. Except it doesn't arrive, and doesn't arrive and doesn't arrive...so, after an hour of waiting, I give up and take a room.

Thursday, February 22

I get up early to get back to the bus depot to catch one of the scheduled morning departures at 7:30, 7:45, or 8:20. None of them arrive. I am very annoyed and frustrated, which I know I shouldn't be. *This is India,* I keep repeating to myself.

There's a train at 9:00, and I ask a guy, "How far to the train station?"

"Don't worry, Madam, bus will be here in a few minutes," he assures me.

Part of me wants to believe him, and another part of me hopes the bus doesn't show just to prove him wrong. Turns out he *is* wrong—since there's still no bus at 8:30. So, I take off to find the train station. Taxi drivers all want an outrageous sum of money. Naturally, the station is farther away than I thought. I'm angrier and angrier with every step. I'm now tired and frustrated, but I get to the station just in time, as a guy tells me the train will arrive in five minutes.

Whew!

Well, it does arrive—an hour later, but at last, I'm on my way to the town of Ernakulum in the state of Cochin. Once there, I set off to find the Tourist Office, which I wrongly assume to be nearby. I walk for an hour and finally end up taking a room back where I started from!

Tired and dirty, I collapse for a while before going out for a lousy lunch. This is definitely not my day. But later, I manage to find the Tourist Office, and they're not closed!

Armed with a fistful of brochures, a much-needed map, and a reservation for a bus tour in the morning, I finally feel accomplished.

Friday, February 23

On this day, I'm learning more real history than I ever did from the nuns back at St. Stephens.

The Portuguese explorer, Vasco de Gama, was the first European to sail to India by going around Africa. His discovery of this new sea route helped the Portuguese establish a long-lasting colonial empire in Asia and Africa, to later be replicated by the British. I'm remembering the history lessons from my childhood which idolized the European explorers and missionaries who conquered, colonized, and converted these "heathen" countries. The guide's commentary is carefully worded so as not to offend the (mostly) westerners on his tour bus, but the point is made. Western countries profited greatly from resources found here.

In the afternoon, I go to the Port Health Office to get the recommended cholera shot. But I'm told to "come back tomorrow," since the doctor is busy.

Oh well, everything was going too smoothly today. Another reminder, *"Marilyn, this is India."*

Saturday, February 24

I go for the cholera shot, where I'm kept waiting for an hour. Finally, someone comes over and asks me, "What are you waiting for?"

Oy!!

Tuesday, February 27: Traveling to Goa

My dog-eared copy of Lonely Planet's *Across Asia on the Cheap* recommends the train which goes inland to Bangalore, but the bus is much cheaper and—on the map—is more direct. Which is why I am on this bone-jarring local bus in the state of Karnataka in southwestern India.

It's a forbidding, scrubby wasteland, unlike any place I've ever seen. Vultures feast on the carcasses of once-holy cows that litter the desolate landscape. Waves of heat radiate off the roadway. It's hotter than hell.

So far in my experience, most Indian buses are packed with passengers hanging out the doorways. But on this desolate route my bus is nearly empty. Up ahead, I see a shimmering black dot on the side of the road. As we approach, the bus slows to a halt and a solitary figure climbs onboard. I assume it's a female, as she is concealed from head to toe in a heavy black burkha. Even her eyes are obscured behind black mesh.

I am mesmerized. In all my travels through Asia, this is my first sighting of a Muslim woman wearing this garb. I'm sweating through my thin cotton blouse and she's standing in the hot sun wearing black from head to toe?

I recall the green wool plaid uniform I had to wear at St. Stephen's. How I hated it!

And I wonder: *Does she hate her uniform? Does she always wear it? Is she allowed out in public without it? Isn't she hot?*

As a western woman traveling alone, I am accustomed to being stared at. Now, I stare. She steals a glance back at me across the aisle. My curiosity is relentless. *How old is she? What does she do? What is her life like? Is she married? Does she envy me?*

*Isn't she **HOT**???*

She catches me staring and she stares back from behind the mesh slit in her head covering. We don't speak. A few more miles down the road, she signals the driver to stop. As she stands, she turns toward me. Behind the veil, I think I see her eyes smile. I smile back. The bus creaks to a halt and she gets off.

I will never forget her.

Sunday, March 4: Arrive Bombay

I spent a few days in Goa—which gets a lot of publicity, but I was unimpressed. I'm not a "beach" person, for starters, since I am not comfortable in a bathing suit. The beaches weren't that great. Lots of Indian tourists and hippies. But I spent only six rupees per night for lodging. And I met two nice Brits from Bombay—Peter and Roland—with whom I hung out quite a bit.

They recommended traveling here to Bombay by ship, and—even though it took twenty-four hours—it was nicer than any of the other modes of transportation I've experienced thus far in India.

I'm excited to get to the General Post Office, since that's where I've instructed family and friends to send correspondence. But I'm terribly disappointed to learn that—for the first time in Asia—somebody decided to get "efficient." They hold letters for only a month and then return them to sender. I'm getting accustomed to disappointment, so I don't let it bother me too much. Hopefully, the Delhi post office won't be quite so efficient.

But there's a lovely valentine from my sister-in-law and a letter from Sheila filled with negative news about mutual friends: One couple is splitting up. Two girlfriends are having issues with each other. And Sheila's job is problematic.

Glad to be here instead of there!

But nothing from my mom, which is a bummer because our last phone call was so emotional.

At the Tourist Office I am overwhelmed by all the options. The question still haunts me: *Should I go home?* But there's so much more to see: obviously the Taj Mahal. And I would love to go to Nepal. And I've heard great things about Kashmir in the north.

So, I decide to buy a thirty-day India Rail Pass.

Wednesday, March 7: Depart Bombay

When I check out of the Stiffles Hotel, the guy wants to charge me 45 rupees per night, instead of the 16 I had expected. I keep my cool and compromise with him—paying 100 rupees for three nights.

I'm purposely taking the night train at 9:15 so I can save money on accommodation. It's 2:30 a.m. when the train arrives in Manmad, where I wait for the 3:50 a.m. train to Aurangabad. It's a chilly, mostly sleepless night but—once again—I'm treated like royalty. The porters fix me a special place to lie down. It's only marginally more comfortable than the floor of the train, where old ladies and mothers with babies fend for themselves to lie down.

I should feel guilty, but I don't.

At Aurangabad, I book lodging at the youth hostel for the night. This is the cleanest, nicest place I've seen in months—and it's only five rupees (about 45 cents). Too bad it's only for one night. I've come to this remote place in order to visit two of India's "not to be missed" attractions, according to my guidebook.

The Ellora Caves are impressive, but the nine-hour tour is way too long for this tired girl. It's hard to comprehend that these caves—thirty-four of them—were carved from a single outcrop of basalt rock with nothing more than hammers and chisels way back in the sixth century. They estimate that it involved removing more than 200,000 tons of rock!

On Friday, I visit Ajanta Caves. Equally impressive, and this time, I have more energy to appreciate the incredible feat and talents of these ancient artisans. These caves are even older than those I saw yesterday, dating back to two centuries BC—that's *before Christ!*

It's one thing to read about these kinds of places from a book in history class (not that I had ever heard of either of these sites)—and quite another thing to stand in awe, witnessing first-hand the artistry, grandeur, and mastery of such an achievement.

Although they were well-known by locals, the Ajanta Caves were "discovered" in 1819 by a British officer on a hunt as he tracked a tiger into a deep ravine. A local shepherd boy guided him to a cave entrance, which was obscured by centuries of tangled jungle growth. And the rest, as they say, is history.

We don't visit all of them, but there are twenty-nine caves with intricate carvings decorating the exterior facades, walls, ceilings, arches, and pillars, with hundreds of masterful sculptures of Buddha through his many incarnations, plus elephants, horses, bulls, lions, nymphs, and meditating monks. Whatever surfaces aren't carved have been decorated with paintings and murals. Some paintings are of monks, hermits, or Buddhist devotees, while others feature handsome noblemen, tiara-adorned princesses, and mostly naked dancing girls in sensuous scenes of love-making and displays of female physical beauty. I'm not surprised to learn that these images shocked the Victorians back then, as well as the religious zealots of today.

Once again, I'm thrilled that Lonely Planet has directed me to a place I'd never heard of. It was way out of my way—but worth it!

Getting out of here—as expected—is as challenging as it was getting here. I take a local bus to the town of Jargon, only to find that there are no reservations available for accommodations in the railway Retiring Room. So, I spend the night (for free!) in the first-class Ladies' Lounge. But it's cold and there is no place to lie down.

Saturday, March 10: En Route to Delhi

It's a twenty-four-hour train ride to Delhi in the third-class Ladies' Compartment. I manage to get some sleep after climbing onto the luggage rack, which a couple of doting old women have cleared for me. I make a mental note that this will be a good story some day!

Sunday, March 11: Arrive Delhi

I find a cheap room near the Main Bazaar area of Old Delhi. As usual, the hotel boys are a nuisance—they mistake my courtesy for attraction and will not leave me alone. I escape from their unwanted attention into the crowded narrow streets around Connaught Place, where I wander into an Indian fast-food restaurant. I'm confounded at the choices when a guy steps forward, introducing himself as a representative of the Tourist Bureau. I follow his suggestion and order Masal Idli, which is a fluffy rice cake with a sauce. Afterward, he invites me to see some sights on his motorbike. He seems nice, and he's good-looking, so I agree.

My mistake. He wraps my arms around his waist to ostensibly hold on, he helps me up and down the stairs when I need no assistance—and is oblivious to my resistance. This has happened so often, and I'm just plain tired of it. *I'm an independent woman and I don't need help!* I thought this guy was more intelligent and would be more perceptive than others who have hit on me. Or maybe he's just being chivalrous, I just don't know anymore.

It has become a battle of wills—and I'm winning. Finally, he drops me back at the restaurant, explaining, "It's too far out of my way to take you back to your hotel."

Fine with me.

Walking back to my hotel, I pass a travel agency that's still open. I take a deep breath and venture inside to make some inquiries.

The travel agent (who is very handsome) helps me plot a route through the parts of India and Nepal that I want to see before I leave. Consulting a calendar, he suggests Iraqi Airways' Thursday night flight from Delhi to London on April 19. That would give me almost six more weeks of travel. The fare is $345. I write everything down and promise to give him a decision tomorrow.

Sitting on my bed back at the hotel, I allow myself a good cry. The freedom, flexibility, and fun I'm enjoying—I don't want it to end! I'm consumed with questions. Should I buy the ticket he suggested? What if I want to stay longer? What if I run out of money? What will the ticket from London back to the U.S. cost me? What will I do when I go back to the States? Will my family and friends understand that I'm a different person? Why am I so bloody indecisive?

As I've done in the past, I decide to decide later. Tomorrow is another day.

I feel better.

Monday, March 12

First thing on today's agenda is the General Post Office where—hooray!—I have mail waiting for me. A letter from Mom is very supportive, saying, "don't hurry on my account." Wow—this is in such contrast to our last phone conversation.

In the afternoon, I spend a few hours at the American Library and read the *New York Times*. I've been away from the States for more than six months—and not much has changed. The same alarming headlines and problems that never seem to get resolved.

I return to the travel agency and commit to the April 19 departure flight. Fingers crossed, everything will work out okay.

Tuesday, March 13: To Agra

The express train arrives here at 9:30 a.m., and I take a rickshaw to the Tourist Rest House where I meet Sophie from Greece in the reception area. We share a room and some nonstop conversation. I guess it's been awhile since I had anyone to talk to!

We go to lunch, to a marble factory, and then to a gem store where I buy two black semiprecious stones that reflect light in a pretty, star-like effect. I'll probably never get the stones set into earrings, but the salesman was so helpful and patient I couldn't leave without buying something from him.

And then—the Taj Mahal! I get shivers and teary eyes at my first glimpse of this magnificent place, which I have only dreamed about. It doesn't feel real. And it doesn't look real, either. Most places don't look like the pictures, but the Taj really is as pretty as the photos. Especially when the sun sets and the full moon rises in the sky…I am speechless. And it's so romantic in the moonlight—I'm wishing I were sharing this experience with someone special. It's the first time I've wanted to be with a man in a long time!

Twenty thousand expert craftsmen and a thousand elephants were employed in construction of the Taj Mahal, the reflective pool, and its gardens over a twenty-two-year period in the mid-1600s.

And the backstory of the Taj is so tragically romantic. The Mughal Emperor Shah Jahan built this as a mausoleum to house the tomb of his favorite wife (he had two others, as was the custom). She died from complications of giving birth to their fourteenth child.

I say she deserves such a monument!

Wednesday, March 14: To Jaipur

It's just after dawn, and—as usual—I'm in the third-class (i.e. cheapest) compartment on the train to Jaipur.

I'm reading a book about the 1947 Partition—when the British finally agreed to pull out of India. Their hastily conceived plan divided British India along broad religious lines—neglecting to consider the challenge of migration, as millions of Muslims lived in what would become Hindu-majority India, and huge numbers of Hindus and Sikhs lived in what would arbitrarily become Muslim-majority Pakistan to the northwest.

In the days, weeks, and months that followed, fifteen million Muslims, Hindus, and Sikhs—each group fearing discrimination—swapped countries in one of history's largest human migrations. Trainloads of people were attacked in horrific sectarian violence.

For a sheltered young woman from the American Midwest, it's shocking to fathom such hatred and violence in the name of religion. I am equally fascinated and horrified by this bit of history I never knew about.

As my train pulls into a station, a young man staggers, breathless, into the carriage. His white cotton kurta is covered in blood. He runs through the car, looking back as if to see if his attackers are following.

I sit panic-stricken on the wooden bench seat. Maybe Mom was right: I shouldn't be traveling alone in such a dangerous country! Strangely, nobody else in the car seems distressed. Some of them are smiling. A few are even laughing.

I'm relieved when the train finally pulls out of the station, and I'm puzzled about what I had just seen. Outside the window, the morning light reveals familiar scenes of India: people squatting near the tracks for their morning "constitutional," a farmer leading his reluctant water buffalo, and a skinny man pedaling a bicycle loaded with two large aluminum canisters.

And there's an unfamiliar scene, too: people wearing typical white cotton kurtas that are smattered with bright colors. Their faces and hair are smeared with orange, yellow, and green. They are smiling and chasing each other with handfuls of colorful powder. I suddenly realize that the man running though my carriage was not covered in blood. It was red paint.

I ask a smiling lady sitting nearby, "What's going on?"

"It's Holi. The festival of spring!"

Ah, yes. I remember reading something in my guidebook about a unique Indian festival that marks the end of winter—an opportunity to repair and renew relationships, and an opportunity for fun and frivolity.

Arriving at my guesthouse in Jaipur, the proprietor cautions me against going out. "You'll be a target," he warns. Apparently, some fanatics decorate unsuspecting foreigners with cow dung and coal tar. I would have liked to join the festivities but instead stay in and enjoy a relaxing afternoon writing letters.

Later, I find a restaurant where I'm joined by two girls and a guy from Britain. It's a strange experience: they wear hip Indian clothes and tons of eyeliner and talk endlessly about their drug use. I don't contribute much to the conversation—I just want to escape. Freaky travelers like these give us all a bad name.

Thursday and Friday, March 15–16: Jaipur

I was looking forward to coming to Jaipur, but so far, I am unimpressed. I read about how colorful it is here—my guidebook described brilliantly colored turbans worn by men and huge hoop skirts worn by the women. But the most colorfully attired people seem to be the tourists. And there are lots of them!

This state, Rajasthan, is named after the fearless warriors—Rajputs—who opposed every invader India ever had. But it feels like that aggressiveness has passed through to the current generation of males, as I find them to be uncomfortably persistent. For the first time in my life, I'm glad to *not* be beautiful. The constant, continual attention would be a genuine hassle.

I see the City Palace and the Amber Palace—but I'm all "palaced" out. The story of the Maharaja and his twelve wives is interesting, however. Their dresses were fashioned from as much as a dozen yards of luxurious embroidered fabric and required that they be carried on sedan chairs by their servants. Since women were not allowed in the Maharaja's palace, whichever wife he wanted to sleep with had to sneak to his bedroom through a secret passageway.

I rent a bike and try to navigate the roadways with what seems like a million pedestrians and cyclists. I've had enough. The overnight train to Udaipur leaves at 8:45 p.m., and I claim a middle berth and manage to get some decent sleep.

I guess I'm getting used to this lifestyle.

Saturday, March 17: Udaipur

It's St. Patrick's Day in lots of places in the world, but not here.

I claim a place in the fifteen-bed dormitory at the Tourist Bungalow. As usual, I'm the only female. I'm tired and on edge—trying to figure out where to go from here. Jaisalmer, to the west—almost to the Pakistan border—sounds interesting. I can pass on its famous fort, but I'm intrigued about the possibility of a camel trek into the desert. However, it's so far out of the way that it'll take a couple of days to get there.

But my mind is made up by an asshole in the dorm who approaches me and uses some obscene hand signals to communicate what he wants from me. Screw him and all the other men in the state of Rajasthan!

I've been all over Asia and never encountered such aggressive, macho men. I'm going back to Delhi as soon as possible!

I go across the street to get a bite of breakfast and meet a guy from California who's a good listener. I pour my frustrations out to him, and it feels good to be heard.

I book a berth on tomorrow evening's train to Delhi.

Back at the bungalow dormitory, I meet another American guy. My lucky day, I guess. Frank is from Ann Arbor, Michigan, but has been employed by a tour company for the past several years. I'm fascinated to learn that he's traveled all over the world and even lived in Honolulu for a time. The company he works for is in Chicago, and I make a note to look into this when I get home. It sounds fantastic, and now that I've got real travel experience, I should be a good fit for such a job!

My mood is noticeably improved from this morning, helped along by some great dinner conversation and Kerala grass that Frank shares with me before bedtime.

Sunday, March 18: Udaipur

They call Udaipur the "Most Romantic City," which might be relevant for anyone staying at the gorgeous Lake Palace Hotel—but I'm underwhelmed.

Frank is good company for the day, and I chat with several other people who have had similar hassles with aggressiveness here in Rajasthan—so I know it's not my imagination. I'll be glad to get back to Delhi where I'm not such a novelty!

Monday, March 19: Traveling by Train

It's an eight-hour train ride to Jaipur, and another seven hours from there to Delhi—so I'm thrilled to get the upper berth of a two-tier sleeper, which is thick with padding. I sleep really, really well.

And the daylight hours provide some fascinating scenes. For many hours, we pass through scrubby, colorless landscape—except for the occasional Rajasthani wearing bright yellow, turquoise, orange, or red. Women wear beautiful flowing skirts and veils, and men are bedecked with expertly wrapped turbans. Camel carts plod along the roadside and proud peacocks strut their stuff, observing the passing scene. Centuries-old walls and forts abound. Out in the fields, crude mud huts are surrounded by harvested cones of golden straw and thatch.

Nobody talks to me or bothers me. I'm in heaven.

Arriving back in Delhi, I wait in a queue for an hour but successfully manage to reserve a seat on a fully booked train to Jhansi on Wednesday.

The rickshaw driver to the cheap hotel on Janpath Lane rips me off by overcharging me, but my dorm bed is costing me only 8 rupees. I tell myself it all evens out in the end.

And he's probably got a big family to feed.

Tuesday, March 20: Delhi

It's a productive day. At the General Post Office, there's a letter from Mom that even includes a few scribbled lines from my dad. Wonders never cease!

I pick up my ID at the Student Travel Office which will get me discounts on future flights. While there, I bump into Anoop, the handsome travel agent who helped me figure out my plans for the remainder of my time in India and Nepal. He books a flight for me

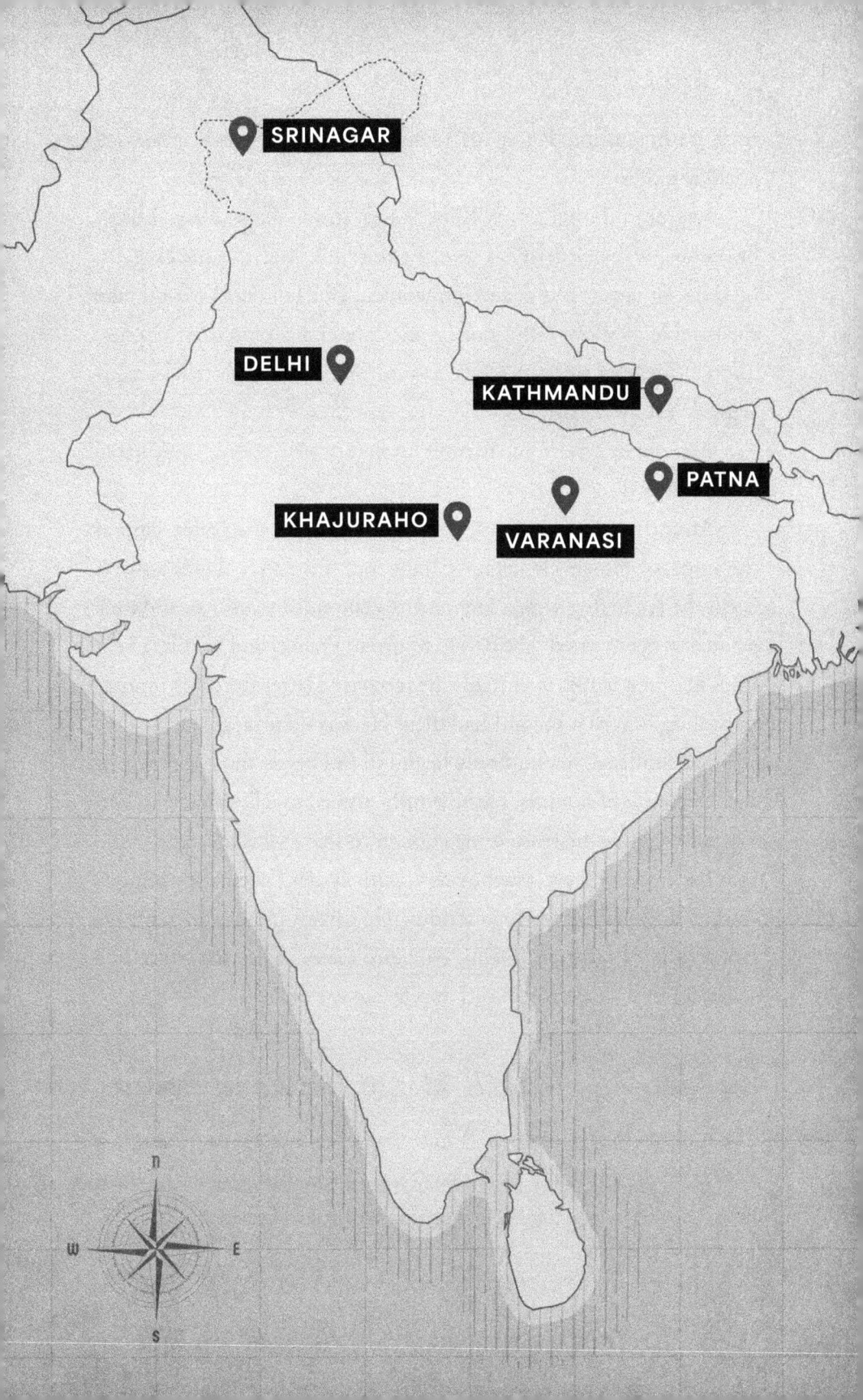

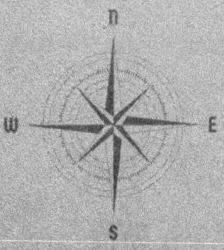

from Kathmandu to Patna, after which he suggests that I come back at closing time.

I agree, although not without reservations. He's so handsome, he's probably married, or has several girlfriends. And, as a travel agent, he certainly meets lots of foreign women. But I'm flattered and take the trouble to shower and put on mascara and my prettiest clothes. Though nothing in my backpack wardrobe could remotely be considered "pretty" anymore.

Anoop takes me home to meet his family, who are very hospitable and kind.

After that, we walk for a while and end up at the coffee shop at the Imperial Hotel. He begins talking and ultimately shares a story: Seems he fell in love with a French girl a couple of years ago, and they wanted to get married. She had to return to France, and he didn't hear from her for a while. Eventually, he received a letter from her mother informing him that the girl had died! He was devastated.

He confided that he'd only begun to feel peace and happiness in the last couple of months. He obviously needed to talk about this, and I'm flattered that he trusted me enough to share with me.

Far from being a playboy as I initially suspected, he's honest, sincere, and maybe a bit *too* serious. He invites me to stay with his family when I return to Delhi. Not sure I should do that, since he's so tender and vulnerable, but I appreciate the offer.

Wednesday, March 21: On the Road Again

The train to Jhansi leaves at 7 a.m. sharp. It's a really fast train, but slow enough to observe lots of bare-assed men squatting in the bush near the tracks—taking their morning bathroom break!

I talk for a while with a nice man from Bangalore—until the Conductor makes him return to his compartment. Then, I meet two British guys, Russell and Mike, heading to the same place as me.

After we disembark the train in Jhansi, it's a hot, dusty, three-hour bus ride to Khajuraho. I appreciate the company of these two guys. Mike is easy to talk to, and Russell could be comedian, he's that funny.

Arriving in Khajuraho, we learn that there's a big dance festival in town. Thus, hotels are crowded and prices are inflated—especially for foreigners like us. I'm used to this, but still find it annoying. The dances are interesting, but our cheap seats are so far away that it's hard to appreciate the talent of the dancers.

Thursday, March 22: Khajuraho

This place is famous for the temples constructed by a breakaway Rajput king between about 950 and 1050 AD. The carvings depict scenes of everyday life of the culture: ladies applying makeup, people writing letters or scratching their butt, farmers plowing the fields, men going to war...all interspersed with sex scenes, which have made this remote place so famous. Beautifully detailed, with perfect proportions and flowing lines, the the explicit carvings depict sex acts—either raw and erotic or loving and tender.

We catch a 4:30 bus to Mahoba, from where we connect with the train to Varanasi which is powered by one of those old steam-driven locomotives. Russell, in his inimitable, audacious style, talks his way to the front—through the more expensive passenger carriages, along the side of the coal car, onto the back of the locomotive—where the engineer is all-too-happy to let these three crazy foreigners shovel coal from the coal car into the firebox on the locomotive. We even get to blow the whistle a few times!

Friday, March 23: Varanasi

Arriving in the holy city of Varanasi, we drop our packs at the hotel and head out to find the famous cremation sites by the River Ganges, fending off the touts and rickshaw drivers who follow us, offering to show us the sights of the city: "Come…this way, Sir, madame…here, please, come…I take you to the burning place."

Eventually, we agree to hire one of the less obnoxious tour guides who is following us. His name is Ayush.

As we get closer to the river, the streets get narrower and more crowded, twisting and turning into a maze of alleyways. I lose all sense of direction—looking left and right at tiny shops, looking down to avoid stepping in cow dung or suspicious puddles, and looking ahead to avoid bumping into something or someone. Many times, I flatten myself against a wall to avoid touching a cow.

Cows are holy in India. I'm still not totally clear about the reason…just as I'm puzzled about why Christians venerate the cross and other symbols. It's got something to do with the fact that cows provide milk, just like a mother. And the religion of Hinduism raises the status of Mother to the level of Goddess—which doesn't equate to the way I see women treated in this culture: relegated (as they are in most of the world) to second-class citizens.

Eventually, we reach a set of broad stairs leading down to the Ganges which is shrouded in haze, looking very mysterious. As far as I can see in both directions, stone staircases lead down to the water. These are the famous ghats.

Ayush explains that there are eighty-four ghats in Varanasi with different purposes. Some staircases lead down from palaces that have been converted to river-view hotels or restaurants. Others are covered in colorful laundry drying in the sun. Many are designated for pūjā—a Hindu ritual whereby flowers or food offerings are left for the divinity. I'm particularly fascinated by the bathing ghats—where people of all ages splash the supposedly holy water of the Ganges on themselves, ostensibly to wash away their sins. Some of the faithful even drink the water, believing that it purifies their soul. I consider it disgusting, since the water is anything but pure and clean. But the faithful believe that the Ganges' water is sacred—and cannot make them sick—because it comes from heaven.

We carefully pick our way down the big stone staircase, equivalent to about three "normal" flights of stairs. Men and women busy themselves along the water's edge, bathing and washing laundry. Out on the river, big rowboats are filled with gawking tourists. I try not to gawk at the holy men, called Sadhus, scantily clad in shades of orange and saffron, with long hair and scraggly beards, their faces covered in ash. They solicit rupees in exchange for a blessing.

Faith is a funny thing.

And then, we arrive at one of the two cremation ghats. I am dumbfounded at one of the most bizarre sights I've ever seen. On a heap of burning wood, I see the head and feet of a corpse as a worker pokes at the charred limbs, pushing them further into the flames. Nearby, a couple of bodies wait their turn, shrouded in orange cloth with marigolds scattered on top.

Ayush tells us that it costs 500 rupees (about $61) to be cremated here at this holiest of places. That is a lot of money, and I assume the owners of these riverside steps are very rich men.

Many old people come to Varanasi to die. It is believed that the dead achieve *moksha*, a liberation from the cycle of rebirth, entering a state of bliss after being cremated here.

It seems disrespectful to watch, but Ayush assures us it's okay. People pass by without taking any notice, heading to other ghats to bathe or do meditation. There are a few people who I assume to be family, but there's no obvious mourning or grieving. Apparently, families traditionally rejoice that their loved one has entered Nirvana.

I think back to the last time I saw a dead person—my Grandma Murphy, lying in an open casket at Deisler Funeral Home in Saginaw. I was not yet six years old, and I thought it weird that she was wearing makeup. She didn't look like the Grandma I knew. The adults were milling about, acting strange. At one point, they all started to cry at the same time—like somebody flicked a switch. I wondered if I was supposed to be crying, too.

But here it's all in a day's work. Tending the fires is a profession for some, and it goes on twenty-four hours a day. After about three hours, the ashes will be collected to be scattered into the waters of the holy Ganges. And poor people collect hot coals for their cooking fires.

Death as a part of life.

Once again, India astonishes me with its uniqueness.

Sunday, March 25: To Patna

I say my goodbyes to Mike and Russell at breakfast and head off to the railway station. My next destination is Nepal, and as usual, I've found the cheapest way to get there. The train is crowded and I find it curious that none of the station names or timings correspond to my schedule. According to the information I got at the station, train #14 left platform #3 at 1:15 p.m.—and I'm on that train. Five hours later, though, the train pulls in at Lucknow, and it's here that I *finally* realize that I'm going in the wrong direction! I've been heading northwest instead of northeast.

But I must be getting acclimated because I remain calm and unflustered. I'm learning!

The Station Master is very helpful. He gets me a berth on the train to Sonepur tonight. I'm getting special treatment and feel a bit guilty…but only a bit. I figure I spend enough foreign currency in this country to warrant some special treatment!

Monday, March 26: En Route to Nepal

Arriving in Sonepur, I catch a crowded local bus to Muzaffarpur, from where I catch another bus to Motihari, where I connect to another bus to the border town of Raxaul. It's 9 p.m., and I'm exhausted and dirty, with absolutely zero patience for the mob of hotel touts and rickshaw drivers that descend on me. I swear at all of them and jump in a rickshaw, instructing the driver, "Take me to the border!" I've no idea if Nepal will be any different, but I just want to get out of this country!

Tuesday, March 27: To Kathmandu

I should have flown.

After the debacle of the last two days, I'd hoped that today—traveling by bus from the plains of India into the foothills of the Himalayas—would be a stunningly scenic journey, as was suggested in my guidebook. Not so.

I'm sitting in the back of the bus, which is a very bumpy ride. It's so dusty that all the windows are closed and the heat is awful. And the dust obscures the visibility so I can't see a thing.

Yup. I should have flown. That would have been a good investment of $45.

But I finally arrive in Kathmandu in mid-afternoon. I spot Brenda, whom I met in Sri Lanka, on the street, and she invites me to share the extra bed in her hotel room.

Finally—something goes right! She's staying in a very nice lodge which has hot water! I take the longest, hottest shower of my life. It's been *so* long since I've had such luxury!

Yeah—I think I'm gonna like this place!

Wednesday, March 28

Yes, I definitely like this place. It's dirty, crowded, and colorful. There are temples, stupas, and palaces at every turn. Colorful markets with lots of tempting stuff to buy. I marvel at the beautifully carved wood door frames and people peeking out from the windows overhead. At 5'1", I'm in good company here, as the residents are very short—as are the doorways. Both men and women wear ethnic attire that are not costumes. For a time, I follow a musical procession of devotees carrying Hindu deities through the narrow, winding alleyways. There are pie shops on Pig Alley selling all kinds of pie—even lemon meringue! And every kind of international restaurant I'd never heard of.

English is spoken everywhere, and I hear familiar rock-and-roll music for the first time in a looong time: The Grateful Dead, Doobie Brothers, Bee Gees, and Deep Purple. I think I'm experiencing culture shock!

Nepal became a favorite destination for hippies a decade ago. For those seeking to escape from a world of war and materialism, it was cool to travel here overland from Europe in a bus or van. Everything was cheap, and marijuana and hash were legal here. Flower children flocked to this spiritual place where, previously, only diplomats and mountaineers ever visited.

An alley near the main square became a meeting place for these free spirits and came to be known as "Freak Street." It's not as freaky nowadays, but I'm grateful it's still cheap and has retained its global vibrancy.

Brenda is leaving tomorrow for Greece, so she's intent on spending her rupees. I'm intrigued by the block prints on rice paper, the chunky jewelry and wood carvings. But I still don't have a ticket beyond London and I have no idea what it will cost, so I must be conservative with my spending.

Thursday, March 29

Brenda departed this morning. I hate being the one left behind—I always feel empty and lonely. It's much easier to be the leaver.

I don't want to get out of bed. I waste most of the day away—reading, doing laundry, and taking a hot steam facial that leaves my face all red and blotchy. But hopefully, it'll help the complexion in the long run.

I sit down and work out a potential budget. There's so many neat things to buy here, but I don't know how much it'll cost me for my remaining twenty-ish days of travel, and how much it'll cost to get myself all the way back home. A crystal ball would be nice right about now.

Friday, March 30: Dhulikhel

Took a ninety-minute bus ride to the small town of Dhulikhel, outside the Kathmandu Valley at about 5,000 ft. elevation. The lodge is a pleasant place to hang, as I've been feeling very lazy and unmotivated. The mountain views in this country have—so far—been disappointing. At sunrise, I can make out a few of the mighty peaks, but they disappear as it gets lighter. Again, as in Kathmandu, there are many foreign travelers here. I meet a couple of British volunteers assigned to a cotton project in the south of the country, who are here getting language training. And ex-Peace Corps volunteers aplenty: two American girls who served in Malaysia and three guys who served in the Philippines.

And then, there are two American students from a "floating university" docked in Madras, India. They flew here to Nepal for a couple of days. The guy is totally obnoxious: money to burn, spoiled rotten, stupid, and insensitive—an embarrassment to my country. The other student, Robin, had worked her ass off to pay for the experience and is much more appreciative. From their conversation about the goings-on onboard their ship, they're obviously young and immature. Or maybe I'm getting old and jaded? I guess I've really grown up in the two years since I graduated from college.

I've got a cold. And now a legitimate excuse to be lazy and unmotivated.

Wednesday, April 4

Back in Kathmandu, I break down and buy the "Long-Haired Goat" rice paper print that I saw on my first day with Brenda. I have not been able to get it out of my mind so I know it's not an impulse purchase. And I enjoy a fabulous piece of apple pie—still warm from the oven! *Mmmmmmmmm!*

Thursday, April 5

I rent a bicycle and ride to Patan, another city across the river. I'm still not feeling so hot, and I'm unimpressed. There are lots of temples here, but I'm burned out on temples at this point. While having tea on the top floor of a pagoda-turned-restaurant, I hear a commotion outside and look out to see frenetic activity up the street. Two long lines of men and boys are pulling on ropes—obviously hauling something very heavy and big. They are having difficulty maneuvering whatever it is around a corner. I get my camera prepped…ready for something spectacular—and it turns out to be a huge log. A bit anticlimactic but more interesting than the temple visit would have been.

Friday, April 6

My last day in country and I have no more Nepalese rupees. There's not much to do that doesn't involve spending money. So, I go up to the rooftop to get some sun and what do I see? MOUNTAINS! *Wow!* They are so close I feel as if I can reach out and touch them. Last night's rain cleared the air. I can only describe them as majestic and awe-inspiring. And I make a pact with myself to return to Nepal to do some trekking one day in the future.

Saturday, April 7: Back to India

My final breakfast in Nepal is greasy French toast. Then, I'm off to the airport to do something I've never done before, and I hope I'm not making a mistake. I nervously spend precious US dollars on whiskey, cigarettes, film, and a calculator at the duty-free area of the airport. Everyone assures me I'll be able to sell everything and make a handsome profit.

It's a short but turbulent flight to Patna, where Bill, an Australian guy I befriended, gets hassled by the guy at Indian Customs for having lots of cassette tapes and no tape deck. I smuggle out his second (illegal) bottle of whiskey for him. We share a room at a cheap hotel and set out to sell our wares and (hopefully) make a killing. I'm glad to be with Bill because I'm very uncomfortable with this sort of activity. I manage to sell the cigarettes for double what I paid, and the whiskey for three times profit. But I think I'm going home with a calculator I don't need.

Sunday, April 8

Waiting on the platform for the overnight train to Jammu, Kashmir, I meet an Israeli named Avi. He's an interesting guy who has spent five weeks at a yoga ashram in Patna. As one would expect from a yoga guy, Avi is easygoing, kind, trusting, and gentle. He's the perfect traveling companion for me right now. But he didn't reserve a berth so ends up sleeping on the floor next to mine. This involves all sorts of discussions and persuasion with every change of Conductor along the route.

Monday, April 9: Arrive Kashmir

It's a beautiful morning as I see mountains, camels, peacocks, and endless wildflowers as we travel north. I'm thinking how supremely happy I am, after spending six months of perfect bliss. Well, it didn't always seem perfect at the time, but looking back, I am so very grateful that my trip has unfolded the way it did. And that it did not happen as I'd expected when I left the States seven months ago.

The train pulls into the station at Jammu at 11 a.m.—almost on schedule. And, surprise! Who is waiting on the platform but Anoop, the travel agent from Delhi.

I'm blown away and, frankly, a bit uneasy to learn that Anoop has traveled here from Delhi to see me and must return tonight. I make awkward introductions, and Avi says goodbye, as he's off to catch the bus to Srinagar—which is what I'd be doing right now if not for Anoop's surprise appearance.

I find a cheap hotel nearby and book myself a room with a somewhat sinister-looking hotel clerk and then buy a bus ticket to Srinagar for tomorrow. Then, we go off to lunch where Anoop mumbles something about "gambling his life" by coming here to meet me.

Oh my god. What have I done? I choose to ignore his comment and make small talk while in the back of my mind I'm desperately trying to figure out how to turn this around.

Over the course of the past few months, I've had plenty of young men suggest that they "wanted me," which I've disregarded with ease and without consequence. I'd been warned by other female travelers that western women are a ticket out of poverty and a means to gain legal citizenship. But I've never considered any of the men I've met on this trip to be "relationship material." I'm having the time of my life: growing, experiencing, and learning about myself, and I am not the least bit interested in getting serious with anyone.

After lunch, Anoop convinces me to change my lodging because he doesn't trust the guy at the other hotel. So, I end up at a place that seems like the Ritz by comparison, where we spend the rest of the afternoon talking and talking. He wants to know everything about my life, my history, my family, and so forth.

After a while, he lays the big one on me: "I love you, Marilyn. Only you. I will never stop loving you, and I am confident that we are meant to love each other. And I'll always be there for you—you can call me anytime during the rest of your life because I'll be waiting for you," etc. etc. etc.

He is *so* dramatic! Obviously, he has watched too many Hindi movies. I've never met anyone who feels so much, so *intensely*. If he wasn't so sincere, this situation would be laughable.

I talk and talk and try to drill into him that he shouldn't waste any chances at happiness waiting for some kind of commitment or assurance from me—because it is not going to come. Ever.

But he continues: "I see you in my imagination, wearing a red wedding sari with gold trim…"

He has *got* to be kidding me! A good Indian wife I will never be! And I tell him so. And, as before, he doesn't hear me.

I glance at my watch and suggest that it's time for him to catch his train back to Delhi. He agrees, reluctantly. I see him to the door and wish him a safe journey. I can tell he's hoping for a hug and kiss, but that is not happening.

I return to my room in a state of utter disbelief at what has just happened. *Marilyn, you are DEFINITELY not in Michigan, anymore!*

Tuesday, April 10: To Srinagar

Early this morning, I get a front seat on the twelve-hour bus to Srinagar and thoroughly enjoy the beautiful panorama at every turn in the road.

Thinking about yesterday, I'm still in utter disbelief.

As the bus finally pulls into Srinagar, who is there to meet me, but Avi! *Geez, Marilyn—you've got a man in every port?*

I'm happy to see his familiar face. And relieved to hear his explanation that he's staying with a family on their simple houseboat. "It probably wouldn't earn even one star in the ratings system, but there's an empty bedroom if you would like to stay there, too," he suggests.

"Absolutely," I say, delighted to avoid the hassle of figuring out where to stay.

The houseboat is old and quaint—like living in grandma's attic. I'm excited that I'll be able to experience family life here. The Muslim family is very gracious, and we share dinner. Noor, the wife of the oldest brother is only twenty-two years old but has been married for eight years! I cannot fathom being married off at fourteen years old! A spunky little sister named Bula-Bula is ten, and I look forward to spending time with her.

I desperately want to sleep, but I'm too polite to decline an invitation from one of the brothers, Nadir, for a ride through the canals on his shikara—Srinagar's version of a gondola. It's peaceful and quiet and we pass many houseboats with signs boasting of their 5-star rating. Many of the "tourist" shikaras are extra-fancy, featuring cushions, curtains, pillows, and hash pipes to mellow out the journey even more.

Wednesday, April 11

Before heading out today, I review the information I've read in my guidebook.

Kashmir and its capital, Srinagar, were a summer escape for the Mughal Emperors from the oppressive heat of the plains. During Colonial days, the Maharajah would not allow the British to buy property. So, the Brits found a creative way around the rule for their summertime visits—they lived on houseboats on the rivers and lakes. Hence the pleasantly old-fashioned ambiance of this place.

However, Kashmir is a major stumbling block in amicable relations between India and Pakistan. The border was arbitrarily established by the British in 1947, dissolving 300 years of colonial rule. The Partition was hastily drawn up on July 18 and ordered that the world's largest empire be divided no later than midnight on August 14. Not surprisingly, it created suspicion and fear, such that millions of people migrated from one region to the other in a panic, with devastating violence and loss of life.

Evidently, the border looks different depending on whether the map was drawn up by an Indian or a Pakistani. Again, religion seems to hurt more than it helps.

Avi and I head to the temple, part of which is more than 1,500 years old. From the top, it's a fine view over the city and the lakes. There are many beautiful gardens which I probably should appreciate more than I do. And we visit a factory where they process wool—and I learn more than I ever knew about what happens after they shear hair off the back of a sheep.

Avi is a nice guy, but he is most definitely not a conversationalist. So, I'm relieved when some foreigners enter the restaurant where we're having dinner. Rita is a lovely thirty-nine-year-old American traveling with her twelve-year-old daughter and an orange-robed character named Sam. Rita is a renowned palmist, Tarot card reader, and fortune teller—which is how she travels around and makes her living.

Typically skeptical of such people, I grow more and more interested as the evening wears on. Eventually, I agree to a Tarot card reading. The restaurant is loud, and I wish I could record our session, but several details stand out. She lays cards on the table in front of me, explaining that three of them are "bad" cards arranged in a triangle. But the card in the middle—the Queen of the World—symbolizes that I've overcome the bad. "You've gone through a lot of emotional changes and relationship uncertainty," she explains. Her reading ends with the Queen of Cups and an accompanying King.

Very interesting! She offers to go deeper, to get at the real nitty-gritty, but I decline, knowing it will cost more than I'm comfortable spending at this point. But I promise myself that someday, when I have money to flit away, I'll pursue this process. I'm probably misinterpreting her explanation, but I kinda like the idea of being "Queen of the World" for a while!

Thursday, April 12

Walking around the city of Srinagar is fascinating. The people are interesting. Young girls are very attractive, in a tomboy kind of way. They have husky voices, and there is nothing shy and feminine about them. Old Muslim ladies wear head coverings and men wear turbans. Children are happy. People seem to be comfortable and content. There's lots of singing. It's easy to smile at them, and I get a big grin in return every time.

I buy a vegetarian cookbook, eager to go home and try to replicate the food I've grown to love.

Beautiful spring flowers are blooming everywhere, reminding me of home. I'm thinking about home a lot these days. One week from today, I'll be headed there.

Nadir takes me and Avi out to the big lake, Dal Lake, to see the "super deluxe" houseboats. They're touristy and commercialized, but very pretty—with crystal chandeliers, lead glass windows, wood carvings, etc. Many advertise as "5-Star Houseboat," and I wonder if I'll ever come back here and afford to stay in such luxury.

Later, we enjoy smoking some hash in the light of a beautiful full moon.

What a great life this is!

Friday, April 13

Ali and I accompany Avi to the bus station, where he's heading to the mountains. As we hug goodbye, Avi assures me that I'm welcome to visit him in Israel.

Then, we go to the house of Nadir's sister and have a fascinating glimpse of family life. There are no men around today—only women and children. The boys are playing with hoops outside, and the girls are hanging around at home, playing and helping with household chores. I fall in love with one little girl with beautiful, expressive eyes and a great personality. I'm very impressed by the amount of affection displayed by all.

I witness a neighborhood squabble unlike any I ever experienced back on Glendale Street. One of the boys accidently steps on a neighbor lady's duck and breaks its leg. The lady then kills the duck and initiates a big discussion with the boy's mother about payment—whether in rupees or another duck. All the neighbor ladies gather around commenting on the situation. Of course, I can't understand a word, but I find it fascinating that there seems to be no hard feelings or animosity. Very healthy!

I enjoy a delicious lunch of mutton with potatoes, onions, and chapatti. Very tasty!

Returning to the houseboat, I notice too late that the board isn't propped securely against the side of the boat, so I take an unplanned dip into the lake! Well—it *is* Friday the 13th, after all! Somehow, I manage to save my purse and camera from dunking. The neighbors get a real kick out of it!

Sunday, April 15: Easter

It's a cold, damp, rainy day, but I go off to find the Catholic Church. I arrive a few minutes late, covered in mud. It's a nice service, and the place is full of people. I can't help but think that next week at this time, I'll probably be back home attending Mass at St. Stephen's. And I hope, I won't be preoccupied with clothes and appearances, as I always was before.

Back on the houseboat, I give small gifts to the girls, Raja, Shama, and Bula-Bula. They're all little things, as I don't have much to give— but they've all been fascinated with my possessions.

Noor tells me later that Shama made a deal with Bula-Bula: she'd do all of her housework in exchange for the necklace I'd given her. Shama is so bright, cheerful, independent, and helpful. She was raised that way—not to be a demanding, helpless child. Noor wants her to be a doctor, and I don't doubt that she'll make a good one.

I'm bummed because the flash attachment for my camera won't work and I have no pictures of this special family.

During dinner, the family gives me a very old silver bracelet. I am touched and sad to be leaving them.

Kashmir has been a poignant and perfect finale to my extraordinary travel experience.

Monday, April 16: Back to Delhi

Early bus to Jammu, which takes most of the day, from where the overnight train to Delhi departs at 9:45 p.m. I've never added up how many hours I've spent in transit. But I've got more time than money, that's for certain!

Tuesday, April 17

I arrive in Delhi at 10:30 a.m., expecting to see Anoop waiting for me on the platform.

Nope. *Must have lost my touch. Maybe he's gotten over me already?*

It's extremely hot here. Whew! Now I know why the Maharajas escaped to Kashmir. And it's an obvious sign that it's time to leave here to return home.

I walk to the Student Travel Office, where Anoop is working and agree to come back later this afternoon when he's off duty.

Passing a sidewalk stall selling my favorite treat, mango lassi…I reluctantly decline, telling myself I shouldn't splurge and spend the one rupee. That's only fifteen cents, but every penny is precious at this point. I have a flight only as far as London. I have no idea how much it will cost to get back to the States from there—and there's no way to know.

At the General Post Office, there are four letters from Mom. She's so excited that I'm coming home. She also wants me to fly all the way into Tri-City Airport because, as she writes, "…your father gets nervous driving into the big city. Plus, it's expensive to park. You managed to travel all around the world, young lady, so I'm sure you can figure out how to get yourself home."

Grrrr. This is infuriating, because that extra flight segment will cost a lot of money which I don't have. Detroit is less than 100 miles from Saginaw—*and my dad doesn't want to drive ninety minutes to meet the daughter he hasn't seen in almost eight months?*

And, "*…it's expensive to park?*" Oh, Mom, if you had ANY idea…!

But admittedly, I've not been forthright with her about my financial constraints because I didn't want to worry her more than she already was. I've never elaborated about the extremely low-budget lifestyle I've been living all these months.

I return to the travel agency when Anoop gets off, and he explains that his family is expecting me for dinner. Oy. But I cannot decline. It's an uncomfortable evening for all of us. His mother is polite, but it's clear to me that she wants her son to marry a nice Indian girl from his caste. Certainly not this wildly independent American.

After dinner, in private, Anoop takes up his familiar litany of love. But the drama's been played out, so it's not as heavy as before. He's written three letters to me—one for every day since he last saw me. They are *so* mushy and flowery. I can hardly believe this is happening to me.

I could probably get rid of him by being rude and obnoxious to the point he'd be disgusted with me. But I truly enjoy his company and keep hoping that some of my positive attitude and energy can inspire him to get over his compulsion with me—and live a happy life. Because he deserves it.

Wednesday, April 18

My last full day in India. I recount my money and discover that I have $100 more than I thought I did. *Hallelujah!*

I set off to sell the film I bought at the Nepal duty-free store, but nobody's interested. *Serves me right for trying to make big profits.* I finally manage to sell it for a loss, but at least I have a few extra rupees instead of film I won't use.

Late this afternoon, I'm biding my time in my hotel room—expecting Anoop to show up after he's finished work. But he doesn't come. An American named Evan has invited me to join him for dinner, which I decide I will do if Anoop doesn't show soon. Evan asks me to join him on the hotel rooftop to share a joint. Why not?

It's really good grass from Kerala, and I am enjoying a very nice buzz when—naturally—Anoop decides to show up.

He explains (as I try to pretend I'm not high), "I was feeling confused and sad, and then I realized that it would be stupid to waste this opportunity to see you."

Anoop takes me to a fancy hotel for a nice dinner, which I'd appreciate more if I wasn't just trying to keep on track with the conversation. But I must be making sense because he seems to be following my train of thought when I dare to speak. And the elegant service is certainly nicer than anything I've had in a long time. I eat way too much!

I'm not sure, but I think there's a possibility that I might be getting through to him. He's agreeing with me on some basic, optimistic philosophies, and he isn't so morose when I give him an indication of the probable outcome of our relationship. I tell him that everything will work out for the best—whatever happens.

Anoop pays me the nicest compliment when he says, "I love to discuss things with you because of your keen intelligence."

Wow. Haven't ever heard that before. He loves me for my mind!

He also tells me that my $345 airfare to London goes up to more than $400 after May 1st, even for people who already purchased their tickets.

Whew!

Thursday, April 19: Depart India

Lots to do before my flight leaves late tonight. I've a long list of things I have been waiting to purchase, and it's fun to shop and spend my wad of remaining rupees on silks, spices, and handicrafts.

Later in the afternoon, I return to the hotel to shower, change, and finish packing. I manage to stuff everything into my backpack and the canvas carry-on that I bought for the flight home. I expect that Anoop will show up, but if he doesn't, I'll take the airport bus at 7:10.

Anoop stops by to explain that he must work late but will meet me at the airport restaurant. I'm wondering what the goodbye will be like. Perhaps worthy of a Bollywood scene?

Sitting on the airport bus, I realize that this is it: I am finally heading home! Seems like a long time ago that I climbed into Dad's green Chevy Impala for the ride to Tri-City Airport. I was a different person back then.

I locate the restaurant and order my favorite Indian meal—dal and chapatti. Anoop shows up just as I'm finishing. I'm happy to see that he's with his friend, Kamal. Maybe his goodbye won't be quite so emotional in front of his friend.

Kamal and I sit and have chai while Anoop takes care of my check-in procedures with the airline. Without revealing too much, I ask Kamal to look after Anoop after I've gone.

Anoop returns with my passport and boarding pass. He kisses me on the cheek and tells me he has clearance to get on my aircraft, where we'll say our "proper" goodbyes. He gives me a letter—"But don't read it till you're at the gate."

I'm introduced to another friend, an employee of Air India, who will shepherd me through the departure formalities without waiting in queues with the "regular" people. I feel like a real celebrity! That is, until I get to Customs, where the agent is very rude. As she's rifling through my bags, I overhear her comment about, "…the stupid things these foreigners buy…"

Damn her! But I keep my mouth shut and I'm waved through to the waiting area at Gate 14. I can see the Iraqi Airways 747 on the tarmac in the distance. A 747—my first double decker aircraft! How exciting this will be!

I settle into a seat and open the letter from Anoop. Amidst his typically gushy, romantic language is a surprise admission—he will *not* be coming on the plane to say goodbye. I'm a little sad, but mostly relieved to be spared the drama, tears, and emotion that this farewell might have entailed. There's a simple silver ring tucked in the envelope. I smile and say a little prayer for him and for his future happiness.

And then they announce the shuttle bus that will take us out to the aircraft. Getting off the bus, I see all the checked baggage lined up on the tarmac. We're instructed to identify our bag and place it on the luggage cart. *How stupid!* It's pitch dark and difficult to see. Obviously, I'm a celebrity no more.

Fortunately, my backpack is easy to spot amidst all the suitcases. I climb the stairs to the plane where there's another unwelcome process—they now want to inspect my hand-carry items…after I've locked everything up!

I guess I'm getting what I paid for.

And one more surprise—there is no seat assignment on my boarding pass! Open seating—on an international 747?

I ask a flight attendant to direct me to the no-smoking section, and she gives me a look as if she's never heard of such a thing.

Oh boy! I guess I'm getting what I paid for.

I turn left toward the front of the plane, where a very assertive French woman is aggressively admonishing everyone that enters that compartment: "No smoking here!"

I'm hanging with her! Her name is Brigit. I grab an empty window seat and am soon joined by an older American man named Edward.

My head is filled with a range of emotions: Relief at the effortless farewell with Anoop, frustration about the boarding process, gratitude to have found Brigit's private non-smoking section, and anxiety about my onward connection in London. Hoping that I'll have enough money for a flight to Detroit. And an expectation that I'll sleep on the floor at Heathrow.

Edward asks probing questions about my journey. He's good for my ego. "You're a gutsy lady," he says, among other complimentary things. He lives in Washington, DC, and I promise to look him up if and when I get there.

Brigit must be very wealthy—she's going to Paris for one day and will then return to Delhi. She's married but has lots of liberty to travel without her husband wherever and whenever she wishes. The other passengers are mostly Middle Eastern men. If any of them dare to light a cigarette in our section, Brigit is on their case immediately.

Not surprisingly, the flight leaves Delhi very late, and I'm nervous that I'll miss the connection in Dubai. However, the pilot announces that Dubai Airport is closed due to the crash landing of a cargo plane, so we're re-routed to a place called Qatar.

Once in Qatar, we're not allowed to deplane as we wait a few hours for passengers to arrive from Dubai. I try unsuccessfully to get some sleep. Funny how I can sleep on a third-class Indian train but can't take a nap in a cushioned airplane seat!

By this time, I have no idea when or how I'm going to arrive in London—and I'm glad to not have a flight booked from there. I'd most certainly miss it at the rate we're going.

It's a good thing I like to fly. Our next stop is Baghdad, where I was supposed to make a connection; but that flight is long gone, so they put me on a flight to Athens. Here, I'm noticing some new things. Almost everyone is a westerner—Caucasians. Lots of fashion plates here and luxury items on display in the duty-free shops. I feel short again but not inadequate.

I'm next routed to Copenhagen. Once there, I'm told my SAS flight to London is overbooked, and there are twenty-five of us on stand-by. I'm not optimistic, but my number gets called! *Woohoo!*

It's only a two-hour flight, but they serve dinner which includes shrimp, cold cuts, paté, and herring. Very Scandinavian. At this point, I have no idea what time zone I'm in, or how few hours of sleep I've gotten since my last hotel night in Delhi. But I'm still upright.

Like I said, it's a good thing I like to fly.

Although I can't rightly claim to have *seen* any of these places, technically, I've added two Middle Eastern and three European countries to my travel resume!

And, in the "small world" department, I'm seated next to a guy who works for the Upjohn company. He's been to Kalamazoo, where I went to college at Western Michigan University! And he listens to my story with fascination. *It feels good to be admired!*

Saturday, April 21: Arrive London

Finally, I've arrived at Heathrow and get some good news. For some reason, I thought I would need to go to Victoria Station in downtown London to purchase an onward stand-by ticket, but since I'm a transit passenger, they can sell me a ticket here. And it costs only 73 British Pounds—less than $160 to Detroit. I'll connect in Washington. My flight is on another 747, and I have an assigned window seat—in the non-smoking section.

I call home collect, and Mom is on pins and needles. I can't resist throwing in a snide remark, telling her, "…my friends are so anxious to see me that they're happy to drive ninety miles to pick me up in Detroit."

I locate an upstairs bar with big plush sofas where I plan to crash for the night. The bathroom is deserted at this hour, so I wash my face and hair in the sink—with hot water!

Sunday, April 22: Arrive Home in Saginaw

I wake up early. The sofa is just a little too plush for comfort. Breakfast is Sugar Frosted Flakes and orange juice. There's an underground tunnel to Terminal 3 with lots of moving walkways. Wall-to-wall carpeting. Ceilings with recessed lights. I must be experiencing culture shock—everything is amazing.

Flying from Washington to Detroit, I am glued to the window—looking at the patchwork of American suburbia: dozens of yellow school buses parked in a row, factory complexes surrounded by acres of parking lots, baseball diamonds, lots and lots of greenery…

The Customs agents at Detroit Airport are noticeably excited by my arrival. Noting the stamps in my passport, they are certain I must be smuggling drugs in the hollow aluminum frame of my backpack. Finding none, they take everything out of the pack. I'm prepared for a body search, but they finally let me go.

Welcome to America!

Once outside, I see my friends Jimmy, Mike, and Denice waving frantically at me. There are lots of hugs and kisses—and then they take me to the bar for vodka gimlets, served by a waitress in a ridiculous costume that barely covers her ass.

Once on the road—the familiar I-75 expressway—Jimmy and Mike are engaged in a discussion about money, the economy, and salaries. I marvel at all the 7-11s we pass. Stopping at McDonald's, I order a cheeseburger and fries. The French fries are as good as I remember, but I'll take dal and chapati over a burger any day.

It's going on 9 p.m. and I'm getting tired—but excited about seeing my family. As we pull into the driveway at 1375 Glendale, I see a big, spotlighted sign on the garage: "Welcome Home, Marilyn!"

Aaawwww. Sweet greetings from my little brother, Ron!

And then, I'm inside, being smothered with hugs, kisses, tears, and more hugs. I can't tell if Dad is serious when he says, "I thought you'd be coming home in orange robes and a shaved head!" Mom doesn't say much, but her smile says it all. I suppose there's no way a mother isn't gonna worry when her only daughter is bumming around—solo—on the other side of the planet for eight months.

My dog, Muttsie, doesn't remember me. Otherwise, nothing seems to have changed.

My girlfriend Sheila arrives, with Barbara. More hugs and kisses. Barbara explains that she's been home for three months and has had a challenging time with her re-entry.

We eat chocolate cake. Wow—it's been a long time since I've tasted anything like it.

Sheila urges me to come along with her—she's got a houseful of people waiting to see me. More hugs and kisses and the unanswerable question, "How are you doing?"

My friends tell me I speak with an accent. And I'm noticing that I am much more assertive with these friends, which is a surprise to me (and to them). I didn't know it had become so natural. *That's a very good thing.*

And I'm continually reminded of my new reality with the oft-repeated question, "What's next, Marilyn?"

Epilogue

I had discovered my passion. I had discovered my confidence.

I didn't know how, or what, or where, but I knew my future would be travel. Now I just needed to discover what would be next for me.

I applied for stewardess jobs. I even got an interview with Northwest Orient Airlines in Minneapolis but didn't get hired. I assumed it was because of my big hips.

I sent my resume to a cousin in Pittsburgh who traveled a lot for business and asked him to share it with the company that handled his corporate travel. It worked. I was hired by the E.F. MacDonald Travel Company in Dayton, Ohio, as an International Travel Specialist in December of 1979.

I loved my job, despite the company's chauvinistic culture. I worked late, and I worked hard. At my annual review, I expected to receive a significant raise, both because of my excellent performance and to keep pace with record-high inflation of more than 13 percent.

That didn't happen. The Vice President, Mr. Connelly, said, "You're doing a great job, Marilyn, but company policy mandates only a 3 percent increase."

The good news: I had my answer. It was time to move on.

I asked a trusted industry supplier (from Michigan!) to recommend "good" companies, because I knew I could probably do worse. I sent my resume to the good ones.

Some weeks later, I got a call from a man in Woodland Hills, California. He owned a small company called Creative Travel Planners (CTP). We chatted. I offered to send him more information—which included a *Saginaw News* article about me and my trip that my proud papa had instigated.

It worked. After two more phone conversations, he sent me an airline ticket for a face-to-face interview. I left Dayton on a dreary March morning in 1981 and landed in sunny Los Angeles after cleansing rains had cleared out the smog and blanketed the surrounding mountains with snow.

Herb had been VP of Sales at Princess Cruises. He drove a cool blue Camaro. He had a big nose and slicked-back Brylcreem hair. He bought me lunch—at Denny's. He was obviously down to earth and no-nonsense. We shared a Midwest work ethic and homespun practicality. CTP was well-respected. Herb and I clicked, and he hired me to be his Director of Planning.

My job involved researching destinations and hotels, negotiating with suppliers, and typing proposals on a Xerox word processor. Herb presented my proposals to prospective and existing clients for their business meetings or incentive trips to reward their top salespeople or best customers. Once a travel program was sold, other CTP employees handled all the operational details.

It was a dream job in a dream city. I was a very happy girl!

And then, four years later, in 1985, Herb called me into his office: "Marilyn, I'm going to retire. And I'm going to sell the company. And I want to sell it to you."

I was speechless. And panic-stricken.

"Me? You want to sell it to *me*???" I protested. "But, but, but … I don't know sales, or marketing, or management, or finance, or…"

122

My thoughts raced: *I have a dream job and he's going to screw it all up? I'm only thirty—much too young! Business owners are men—not girls like me! I don't know how to run a business, or read a financial statement, or...*

"You can do it, and I'll help you," he insisted, interrupting my negative thoughts.

How could I refuse?

With his coaching and an outstanding team of employees, I succeeded. Early on, I made big decisions, like investing $2,400 in the latest technology—a fax machine. I hired people, and I painfully let them go if they were the wrong fit. Existing clients didn't balk at the new ownership, and new customers came from referrals. Suppliers were eager to do business with us. I paid the rent, salaries, and business obligations—on time. And sometimes, I paid year-end bonuses, too. At one point, I changed the company name to the CTP Group because it sounded more professional. The acronym, CTP, stood for Connection, Travel, Purpose—consistent with my worldview.

Year after year, despite my doubts and fears and screw-ups, I was succeeding. Year after year, I savored the lavish hotels and extravagant experiences that our corporate customers expected.

But as much as I enjoyed Rome, Paris, London, and other popular, well-traveled destinations, I yearned to show my customers the more exotic places that had been such a significant part of my origin story. I badly wanted to give them culturally enriching, purposeful, authentic experiences like those that had inspired and transformed me years before.

In the early 2000s, a corporate client had an adventurous streak, and decided he wanted to reward his top salespeople and most valuable customers with a trip to India.

India!! I was euphoric!

That return journey to India was magnificent, and *so* very different than my low-budget experience of years before. The group stayed in luxury hotels that were former palaces of the maharajas. We played elephant polo. We arranged a private cruise on the sacred River Ganges to witness evening prayer ceremonies. Everything was top-notch and exclusive.

But several days into the journey, I started getting feedback from travelers: "We'd rather not shop at that fancy emporium store where all the tourists go. Please take us to the market where the local ladies buy their silk saris."

And when our air-conditioned motorcoach was snarled in traffic—held up by a parade of jubilant young people, musicians, and painted, bejeweled elephants—my travelers spontaneously exited the bus to join the procession, smiling and dancing with the locals in the streets of Jaipur.

I was thrilled to see evidence that Americans, traveling in 5-star luxury, could still desire to step out of their comfort zone to connect with the people of the real India.

Months later, I woke up in the middle of the night, dreaming about India. I sat upright in bed and exclaimed, "WOW!"

And my next thought: *"Oooh, that's a good name for a company!"*

Such was the inspiration for my new leisure division, the WOW! Travel Club, which would offer carefully curated tours to wondrous, less-visited destinations. I would attract like-minded travelers, desirous to explore some of the planet's most beautiful places and meet its extraordinary people. Small-group journeys would include unforgettable "wow" experiences and surprises. And, just as I had discovered as a young traveler, my customers would realize that *those people*—who seem so foreign and strange—are just like us!

Together, we'd discover our common humanity…our connection.

It was, literally, the culmination of a dream. I made plenty of misguided decisions at first, but my WOW! division took hold and became my proudest professional achievement. Those trips were magical—both for me and for my travelers. I loved doing all the pre-trip planning and organizing, and then, during the journey, I'd stand back and witness the spontaneous "wows!" that would bubble up when people were surprised and delighted.

And then, in 2020, COVID shut it all down. Nonessential travel simply stopped for everyone, everywhere.

It was time for me to stop, too. I was sixty-five. Thoughts of retirement had begun to creep into my consciousness. My trusted Vice President, Gabriel Haigazian, was poised and more than ready to take on the challenge of ownership.

So I let go.

But I didn't stop traveling. As soon as the world opened up again, I traveled for fun and for philanthropy. And, late in 2023, I joined a WOW! Travel Club adventure to Thailand. Traveling as a WOWee was an absolute delight! There was never any doubt, but I got to experience first-hand how the business is thriving under Gabriel's leadership. My legacy is intact. My heart is full.

And I've *finally* published this long-planned memoir. A portion of the proceeds from the book you are holding will fund travel scholarships for deserving young students to go abroad to study or do service projects. I envision that the kind of life-defining travel that nourished my soul as a young woman will continue to transform and inspire young people before they succumb to societal pressures of advanced degrees, relationship commitments, mortgages, children, and the other trappings of adult life.

I hope my story has stirred something inside you; aroused your curiosity and fired your imagination. Despite the negative headlines, there is *so* much good to experience in "other" people and places. You need only venture outside your familiar bubble to discover both the treasures of the world—and the treasures of self.

What's Next?

Are you inspired? Motivated to travel? To travel differently and deeper and more intentionally?

I hope so.

Where to begin? (Because it can be overwhelming…)

I'm sharing a handful of recommendations. Please, do your research, trust your intuition … but go. Just go. You'll never regret it.

For the traveler:

The WOW! Travel Club
www.wowtravelclub.com

Indian Experiences (Discovering India Differently)
www.indianexperiences.co.uk

Elevate Destinations
www.elevatedestinations.com/the-elevate-ethos

For the student:

Fund for Education Abroad
https://fundforeducationabroad.org/

For the philanthropist:

Global Volunteers
https://globalvolunteers.org/

Together Women Rise
https://togetherwomenrise.org/learn/travel/

www.ingramcontent.com/pod-product-compliance
Lightning Source LLC
Chambersburg PA
CBHW020204090426
42734CB00008B/939